VEGETABLE GARDENING

2 BOOKS IN 1:

THE COMPLETE COLLECTION TO EASILY GROW VEGETABLES AT HOME

Bradley Gray

Text Copyright ©

All rights reserved. No part of this guide may be reproduced in any form without permission in writing from the publisher except in the case of brief quotations embodied in critical articles or reviews.

Legal & Disclaimer

The information contained in this book and its contents is not designed to replace or take the place of any form of medical or professional advice; and is not meant to replace the need for independent medical, financial, legal or other professional advice or services, as may be required. The content and information in this book has been provided for educational and entertainment purposes only.

The content and information contained in this book has been compiled from sources deemed reliable, and it is accurate to the best of the Author's knowledge, information and belief. However, the Author cannot guarantee its accuracy and validity and cannot be held liable for any errors and/or omissions. Further, changes are periodically made to this book as and when needed. Where appropriate and/or necessary, you must consult a professional (including but not limited to your doctor, attorney, financial advisor or such other professional advisor) before using any of the suggested remedies, techniques, or information in this book.

Upon using the contents and information contained in this book, you agree to hold harmless the Author from and against any damages, costs, and expenses, including any legal fees potentially resulting from the application of any of the information provided by this book. This disclaimer applies to any loss, damages or injury caused by the use and application, whether directly or indirectly, of any advice or information presented, whether for breach of contract, tort, negligence, personal injury, criminal intent, or under any other cause of action.

You agree to accept all risks of using the information presented inside this book.

You agree that by continuing to read this book, where appropriate and/or necessary, you shall consult a professional (including but not limited to your doctor, attorney, or financial advisor or such other advisor as needed) before using any of the suggested remedies, techniques, or information in this book.

Table of Contents: Vegetable Gardening for Beginners

INTRODUCTION 13

CHAPTER 1: WHERE TO START? 18
Clearing Your Garden Spot 18
Killing Weeds and Aggressive Grasses 19
Analyzing and Improving Your Soil 21
Increasing the Soil's Nutrient Content 25
Mulching 26
Composting 27
Essential Tools For Vegetable Gardening 28
- *Watering Hoses and Cans 32*
- *Hand Trowels 33*
- *Hand Cultivators 33*
- *Spades and Shovels 34*
- *Garden Forks 35*
- *Garden Rakes 35*
- *Buckets, Wagons, also Baskets 36*

CHAPTER 2: WHAT IS THE BEST SOIL? 39
Soil 39
Types of Soil 41
- *Clay Soil 41*
- *Sandy Soil 41*
- *Silty Soil 41*
- *Peaty Soil 42*
- *Chalky Soil 42*
- *Loamy Soil 42*

Fertilizing 43
Benefit Of Composting 45
Types Of Composting 48
- *Backyard Or Onsite Composting 48*
- *Compost Tea 49*
- *Leaf-Mold Tea Or Green Manure Tea 50*
- *Vermicomposting 50*

    In-vessel Composting *51*
    Grub Composting *52*
    Cockroach Composting *53*
    Aerated (turned) windrow composting *54*

CHAPTER 3: THE "LASAGNA" METHOD 58
  ADVANTAGES OF A LASAGNA VEGGIE GARDEN 60
  BUILDING A LASAGNA GARDEN 62
  PLANTING GUIDE 73

CHAPTER 4: EASY TO GROW PLANTS FOR BEGINNERS 78
  BEANS 79
  BEETS 79
  BROCCOLI 80
  BRUSSELS SPROUTS 81
  CABBAGE 81
  CARROTS 82
  CAULIFLOWER 83
  CUCUMBERS 83
  EGGPLANT 84
  KALE 85
  LETTUCE 86
  PEAS 87
  PEPPERS 88
  POTATOES 89
  PUMPKINS 89
  RADISHES 90
  SPINACH 91
  SWISS CHARD 91
  SWEET POTATOES 92
  TOMATOES 93
  WINTER SQUASH 93
  ZUCCHINI/SUMMER SQUASH 94
  HERBS 95
    Garlic *95*
    Onions *98*
    Basil *102*

    Cilantro *105*
    Mint *107*
    Parsley *110*
    Rosemary *112*
    Sage *115*
    Thyme *117*

CHAPTER 5: COMMON PROBLEMS AND HOW TO AVOID THEM 121
    ABIOTIC PROBLEMS 122

CHAPTER 6: USEFUL TIPS 130
    PEST AND DISEASE MANAGEMENT 133
    METHODS OF PEST CONTROL 135
    NATURAL METHODS OF PEST CONTROL 139
        Organic Method *140*

CONCLUSION 144

Table of Contents: Companion Planting for Vegetables

INTRODUCTION	**150**
CHAPTER 1: WHY COMPANION PLANTING?	**156**
Why Use Companion Gardening?	157
Structural Support	*158*
Nitrogen Fixing	*159*
Attracting or Repelling Insects	*159*
Allelopathy	*160*
Increasing Yield	*160*
Aesthetics	*161*
Companion Planting Strategies	161
Full Sun vs. Partial Shade	163
CHAPTER 2: THE BENEFITS OF COMPANION PLANTING	**168**
Hedged Crop Yield	168
Helper Interaction For The Crops	169
Protection Of Weaker Plants	170
Suppression Of Pests Without Chemicals	171
Trap Cropping	171
Pattern Disruption	172
Organic Gardening	173
Reduce The Crowding Of Crops	173
Low maintenance of the garden	173
Nutrient Management	174
CHAPTER 3: COMPANION VEGETABLES	**175**
Asparagus	176
Beans	177
Bush beans	178
Pole beans	178
Broad beans	179
Beets	179
Broccoli	179
Cabbage	180
Carrots	181

CAULIFLOWER	182
CELERY	182
CHARD	183
CORN	183
CUCUMBER	184
EGGPLANT	184
HORSERADISH	185
KOHLRABI	186
LEEKS	186
LETTUCE	187
ONIONS	187
CHAPTER 4: PERFECT COMBINATIONS	**190**
CHAPTER 5: VEGETABLES WITH HERBS	**194**
CHAPTER 6: INSECTS IN THE GARDEN	**204**
GOOD INSECTS	204
Ladybugs	*205*
Spiders	*206*
Ground Beetles	*207*
Parasitic (Braconid) Wasps	*208*
Damsel Bugs	*209*
Green Lacewings	*210*
Soldier Beetles	*212*
Tachinid Flies	*213*
Hoverflies	*214*
Predatory Mites	*215*
Solitary Bees	*216*
BAD INSECTS	218
Aphids	*218*
Asparagus Beetles	*220*
Cabbage worms and Cabbage Loopers	*221*
Caterpillars	*222*
Colorado potato beetle	*223*
Flea Beetles	*224*
Mealybugs	*224*
Mexican bean beetle	*225*
Japanese Beetles	*225*
Scales	*226*

Thrips *226*
Tomato Fruitworms (Corn Earworms) *227*

CHAPTER 7: HOW TO START COMPANION PLANTING   230

COST, MATERIALS, LOCATION, AND TIME 230
COMPOST AND SOIL MAINTENANCE 232
CREATING GARDENS IN LIMITED SPACES 234
LOCAL CLIMATE CONDITIONS AND WHAT TO GROW 235
DIFFERENT METHODS 236
The Three Sisters *236*
Square Foot Gardening *237*
Container Gardening *238*
ALLELOPATHY: THE CHEMICAL ABILITIES OF PLANTS 239

CHAPTER 8: GARDEN TECHNIQUES   243

HOW TO FERTILIZE YOUR PLANTS 244
WATERING YOUR VEGETABLE GARDEN 246
WEEDING YOUR GARDEN 249
SET UP SHADE 250
ADD MULCH TO YOUR GARDEN 251

CHAPTER 9: THE KEY TO SWITCHING TO COMPANION PLANTING   253

INSECTS 253
NUTRIENTS 255
STRUCTURAL SUPPORT 256
EXTENDED HARVEST 257
TRANSITIONING TO A COMPANION GARDEN 258
Adding Companion Plants to an Existing Garden *258*
More Tips for Transitioning to Companion Planting ... *261*

CHAPTER 10: MISTAKES TO AVOID   264

STARTING TOO BIG 264
NOT PREPARING YOUR SOIL 265
ESTABLISHING PLOTS IN SHADY AREAS 266
EXCESSIVE WATERING 267

CONCLUSION   270

VEGETABLE GARDENING FOR BEGINNERS

THE BEST TECHNIQUES AND SECRETS TO EASILY GROW VEGETABLES AT HOME

Bradley Gray

Introduction

Vegetables are good for you, good for the planet, and tasty, too.

Growing your own vegetables can be very rewarding and is a rewarding skill for your children to learn. A kitchen garden is also a great way of reducing your food bill.

As someone who came from an agricultural family, I am passionate about the benefits of gardening and know that it will be a life skill that your children will always be proud of.

I like to grow most veg in containers at home for ease and this reduces gardening maintenance while still allowing the chance for great harvests.

Vegetables are best grown in a sunny spot in the garden, as they love sunshine and warmth, or in containers close to your kitchen door so you can use them more regularly.

In this book, I'll show you how to grow your own tasty vegetables.

I want you to know that you can also grow your own vegetables even if you have a small space and not a lot of money to invest.

There's really no reason for you not to grow your own vegetables!

Saving money on your food bill and raising your self-sufficiency levels are just two of the benefits of growing your own food.

Vegetables make a great hobby whatever you want to do. - If you an interested in making money from growing then this book shows you how to build up organic vegetables to sell at the market or join the local community growing scheme. - If you just want to grow for personal satisfaction or, if you are keen to teach the children about how things grow and that healthy food comes from the land, then this is also a rewarding hobby.

For those who already have a garden at home, but don't have any real experience of either gardening or growing, cottage gardens are a good option as they are reasonably easy to maintain.

If you have children but your garden is too big for you to look after effectively then container gardening should be a better option for you as it allows you more control over space and soil preparation.

Vegetables grow in all sorts of weather and soil types so everyone can get involved in growing fresh organic produce.

Growing parsley from seeds is one of the easiest things you could possibly do, there is no need to buy seedlings, just simply gather some seeds from the parsley you have been eating and plant them in a sunny spot outside or in a greenhouse. You could also start some indoors on a windowsill if you are short of time or want to be sure that you have fresh parsley all year round.

Growing vegetables on your own might be difficult in the beginning but don't worry, this book will guide you through the process.

If you are just starting out then feel free to start with the easiest vegetable that is also cost-effective at the same time – garlic, after all, it's so easy to grow and it grows well in containers.

For those who have some experience of gardening already, then there are many other wonderful methods of growing vegetables besides container gardening such as in a greenhouse or even outside in just a small garden patch.

Let us begin.

Chapter 1: Where To Start?

Clearing Your Garden Spot

The first step is cleaning up space so the soil will not be hard to work on. One can clear your garden space any time of the year, but the most optimal is the season before you plant.

1. Outlining the spaces of your garden plot where clearing is needed.

Outlining the areas depend on how you want the plots to be shaped. Try to follow these straightforward guidelines:

If you want the edges of a rectangular or square plot straight, stretch a cord in between the marked line and sticks with white limestone that is ground, which is easily accessible at garden stores.

If you are seeking a circular garden, utilize a rope or hose to outline the area, and ensure that you are fixing the stature to create a leveled curve.

2. Start by clearing the surface. To do this, you will be razing the plants, bushes, weeds, and rocks. Use a mower if you want to cut the weeds and grass near the surface.
3. Dig out the roots of tough weeds and small trees using a hoe, shovel, or pickaxe.

Killing Weeds and Aggressive Grasses

Weeds are the bane of beautiful gardens. Even when you have cultivated a proper garden, you need must weed it from time to time. Be that as it may, weeding is especially important when you are preparing your garden for the first time.

When preparing a garden, you must get rid of the grass and the weeds as much as possible. Depending on the size of the garden, this process can take quite some time to complete.

You can eliminate weeds and active grasses using two ways described below:

Sifting and Digging by hand: In the case of a minute garden digging up the entire earth and cautiously sifting the soil must be done. Carefully remove root and sod parts that might grow up the following year as weeds.

Put a Covering: An easy and chemical-free technique to clear your garden is to cover it with cardboard, clear or black plastic, even old rugs. The existing plants cannot stand these drastic conditions, such as lacking light from the sun and energy, so they eventually die after a month or so.

The plastic rolls can be bought from the home improvement centers and hardware stores. It is necessary that you use the thickest cardboard or plastic. Controlling weeds and grasses by applying covering to your garden spot is straightforward if you follow these steps:

Spread the covering over your entire garden spot, safeguarding the edges with auxiliary rocks, boards, or bricks.

After a month, remove the covers and cut off any grass or weeds with the aid of a shovel. Try to cut at the root level (just underneath the soil surface). If they aren't too thick, a rototiller can be employed.

Analyzing and Improving Your Soil

After you have cleared your garden, the next major step is to have a close look at your soil; give it a hard squeeze, have it checked and tested, improve it, and then work it out to ensure that it is in good shape. Healthy soil gives vegetable roots a balance of all the things they require viz. moisture, air, and nutrients. If you know your soil type, it enables you to neutralize problems that you may face when working on your piece of land.

Testing your soil

Vegetables are kind of fussy about soil chemistry. Excess of a particular nutrient or lack of a particular nutrient, and you have complications.

The quality of the soil is pivotal to the health of the plants. While testing the soil, you need to check for its pH value and make the necessary amendments. You also need to check the drainage of your soil. To do so, you should soak the soil by hosing it down. Let the area remain undisturbed for a day. The next day, take a handful of the soil and squeeze it hard. If you find that water is streaming out of your hand, it means that the drainage of the soil is poor. You should add organic matter or compost for better drainage. Alternatively, you may want to invest in raised beds.

Now, you should check the soil by opening your hand. If you find that the soil has not balled up or the ball breaks down at the slightest touch, the soil may be too sandy. On the other hand, the ball may not break down even if it is poked hard. This denotes that the clay content is high. In both of these cases, you should be adding organic matter. This will improve the texture of the soil and make it suitable for the growth of the plants.

If the ball breaks down when poked, the conditions of the soil are just perfect for plant growth. This is the property of loam soil.

The exact pH enables vegetables to utilize nutrients from the soil. If your soil's pH is not within the specified range, plants can take up the nutrients such as phosphorus and potassium even if they are abundant in the soil. On the other hand, the solubility of certain minerals like manganese may increase to toxic levels if the pH is extremely low.

Most vegetables prefer a slightly acidic environment (pH ranging between 6 and 7) for their optimal growth.

The only way to assess whether your soil is fit for your vegetables is to test it. Don't panic, analyzing your soil is not complex. Here are the two methods to test your soil:

Use a do-it-yourself kit: If you want to access the acidity or alkalinity of your soil, the basic pH test kit can be utilized, available at a nursery. This kit can sometimes assist in calculating the major nutrient content. However, the test only gives you a rough estimate of the pH and nutrient levels in your soil.

Contact a soil lab to do a test for you: A comprehensive soil test might turn out to be a good investment as a soil lab can thoroughly examine your soil. Soil labs don't charge you a lot. Your local

Cooperative Extension Service office or private lab can conduct a comprehensive and reliable soil test. It gives you further insight into your soil; here is what you will know in addition to the pH level:

Since we have seen how to analyze the soil, we will now turn our attention to ways of improving the soil.

To grow plants properly, you need to ensure that the soil is the right one for them. Most plants need the soil of neutral pH, but some tend to require alkaline or acidic soils. Whatever be the type of soil you have; it is possible to modify it so that it becomes more suitable for the plant you wish to grow. However, the steps you take will not have an everlasting effect. Unless you are planning to undertake the steps regularly, you should try using the soil that you have.

Adjusting soil pH

To increase the alkalinity of the soil, you can add ground lime. For increasing the acidity, you can use Sulphur or aluminum Sulphate. All Cooperative Extension Service offices, various lawn and garden centers, and many soil labs have charts showing the quantity of lime and sulfur to be added to fix the pH imbalance. You first have to measure the area of your vegetable garden; the chart tells you the quantity in pounds to be added per 1,000 square feet.

Increasing the Soil's Nutrient Content

If you discover that your soil has a low amount of nutrients, you should add some organic matter to it. Manure and compost can enrich the soil while improving its texture. You can also use organic mulches such as deciduous leaves, straw, and dried grass clippings. These mulches can break down and provide the soil with organic nutrients and improve the soil structure at the same time.

Perfect loam soil is rare, so don't worry if you are deprived of it. To fix your grimy clay or loose sand, you need to add organic matter. You can't change your type of soil altogether, but supplementing organic matter makes your soil more like loam, which is impeccable for vegetable roots. Even if you are lucky enough to have loam soil, adding organic matter to your soil every year will further increase productivity.

Organic matter improves the garden soil as it assists loosening and provides proper ventilation to clay soil. It enhances the water and nutrient-holding capacity of sandy soil.

Organic matter attracts vital microorganisms, beneficial fungi, worms, and other soil-borne organisms that enhance the health of your vegetables.

Mulching

The importance of mulching should never be underestimated. It can insulate the soil and thereby keep the roots of plants safe from extremes in temperature. It can also enable the roots to remain moist by retaining water. More importantly, mulching can curb the growth of weeds in your garden.

Various kinds of mulch can be used. You can purchase a range of them at stores. Some of them are specially created to solve certain specific issues in a garden. However, for general purposes, you can easily make mulch at home.

You simply need to gather all dead organic matter in your gardens, such as dead leaves and broken branches. Your garden itself will yield enough plant matter for use as mulch. Collect this organic matter throughout the year in a designated area and break them down into small particles with machines or by hand. Let the mulch remain all winter. The following spring, you will have enough mulch for use in your garden.

Composting

Compost is regarded as the best organic material to supplement your soil. Composting simply breaks down the waste material into a brittle soil-like material called humus. It is easily accessible and pretty straightforward to use.

Compost is basically decayed organic matter. It acts as a natural fertilizer for your garden. It can be an excellent addition to all kinds of soils. You can easily purchase compost at a low cost, even in bulk amounts. On the other hand, you can make your own compost at home for the garden.

There are many other organic matters such as sawdust and manure that can be employed, but compost has surpassed all these organic matters. Using other organic matters except compost can cause problems. For instance, sawdust undoubtedly adds value to your soil upon converting into humus, but when it decomposes, it deprives the soil of nitrogen. It gives rise to the problem of adding more fertilizer to compensate for the effect. In case you are using livestock mature, it will replenish the nitrogen level of the soil, but the abnormal growth of weeds can be observed as livestock diet consists of abundant hay that contains plenty of weed seeds.

It is always good to use fully composted organic matter; that is prepared for a year or two, so it is decomposed completely, and the salts are drained off properly. Too much salt in the soil can be detrimental to plants. Good quality compost and completely decomposed manure should have a dark brown appearance, earthy odor, and have minute original material evident.

Essential Tools For Vegetable Gardening

Many of all the things that you need are likely already around your home -- particularly if you're working on other outside jobs. Here's a brief list of some helpful vegetable gardening equipment:

 ✓ Gloves allow you to grasp resources better and help you avert hand blisters. Cotton gloves would be the most affordable, but the expensive creature gloves -- made of sheep and goat skin -- last longer.

✓ An excellent straw hat with venting prevents the sunshine from your skin and allows air to move through and cool your mind.

✓ An excellent pocketknife or set of pruning shears is excellent for cutting edge strings and blossoms.

✓ Sturdy rubber boots, garden clogs, or function boots repel water and supply aid for digging.

✓ Bug repellent and sunscreen keep you comfy and secure while working in the garden.

Freezing, Drying, and Canning Veggies

You can conserve vegetables in three distinct ways -- by drying, freezing, or canning them to help your crop last more than if you saved your veggies fresh. I really don't have enough room to explain all the details about these different procedures, however, the following list provides you a thumbnail sketch of each method:

✓ **Freezing:** This is likely the simplest way to conserve vegetables. But if you would like, simply puree up some berries, place them in a container, and toss them in the freezer and they'll last for 4 weeks. The mixture is very good to use in skillet or soups. Blanching is the practice of dunking the vegetables in boiling water for a moment or 2 and then putting them into ice water to cool them off. You then wash the veggies with a towel and then suspend them in labeled plastic freezer bags. Straightforward.

✓ **Drying:** This technique could be rather simple, but it has to be performed correctly to avoid spoilage. Essentially, you dehydrate the veggies by placing them out from the sun to dry, by slow baking them in the oven, or using a commercial dehydrator, which you can purchase in most mail-order catalogs (see the appendix). In hot, sunny climates such as California, you are able to dry 'Roma' tomatoes by slicing them in half and placing them out in sunlight onto a display. Spoilage is obviously an issue, therefore before drying out your veggies, you might have to find some extra info. You usually will need to keep dried veggies in airtight containers; lidded jars work well. You may use dried veggies to create soups and sauces.

✓ **Canning:** Of preserved vegetables, I enjoy the flavor of canned berries the ideal. Nothing tastes better in the midst of winter. But canning is a fragile and labor-intensive process that could require paring, sterilizing jars, cooking, boiling, and also lots of additional work. I typically put aside an entire weekend can tomato and other veggies. I really don't wish to dissuade you, but you want some great recipes, some particular gear, and likely some assistance if you would like to can vegetables.

Placing Off Your Vegetables

You have two options when you harvest your plants: Eat the veggies straight away or keep them to use afterward. Particular veggies need different storage requirements to preserve their freshness. These states can be outlined as follows:

✓ **Cool and dry:** Ideally, temperatures must be between 50° and 60°Fahrenheit, with 60% relative humidity -- states that you usually find at a two-bedroom cellar.

✓ **Cold and dry:** Temperatures must be between 32° and 40°, together with 65% humidity. You may attain these requirements in many home refrigerators or in a cold basement or garage.

✓ **Cool and moist:** Temperatures must be between 50° and 60° with 90% humidity. You're able to store vegetables in a trendy kitchen or cellar in perforated plastic bags.

✓ **Cold and moist:** Ideally, your storage space needs to be 32° to 40°, together with 95% humidity. You are able to make these requirements by putting your veggies in refrigerated bags (veggies in luggage without venting are very likely to hamper quicker) and keeping the bags in a fridge.

Watering Hoses and Cans

Plants need water to grow, and when Mother Nature is not cooperating, you want to water frequently. For a huge garden, you might require fancy soaker hoses, sprinklers, and drip irrigation pipes. However, for many small house gardeners, a very simple hose and watering can perform. Rubber hoses are a lesser chance to kink than nylon or plastic pads, but they are normally much heavier to maneuver around. Whatever material you choose, make sure you acquire a hose that is long enough to reach plants in every area of your garden without needing to take water around the beds to reach far-off plants. Decide on a hose that includes brass fittings and a washer incorporated into the hose; those components make the hose not as likely to fail after prolonged usage. Watering cans can be made from easy, cheap, brightly colored plastic or high-end, fancy metal. Vinyl is lighter, but galvanized metal is rustproof and much more appealing. Watering cans come in various sizes, so try several out for relaxation before purchasing. Ensure it is simple to eliminate the sprinkler head, or improved, for cleanup.

Hand Trowels

Hand Trowels are crucial for digging in containers, window boxes, and little raised beds. The wider-bladed hand trowels that can be brightly shaped and round the conclusion, are simpler to use to loosen dirt compared to narrower bladed, V-pointed ones, these thinner blades are better for grinding tough weeds, like dandelions.

Hand Cultivators

A three-pronged hand cultivator is a useful tool to split up dirt clods, straightforward seedbeds, and also operate in granular fertilizer. Additionally, once you plant your little container or elevated bed, the weeds will come if you want it or not a cultivator functions as a fantastic tool to eliminate these youthful weeds as they germinate. When you are digging a planting hole, then a hand cultivator divides the ground more readily compared to a hand trowel. Much like a hand trowel, make certain to opt for a hand cultivator that feels comfortable on your hands which includes a grip firmly fastened to the blade. The steel-bladed kinds will be the most lasting.

Spades and Shovels

Spades and shovels are just two of the most widely used gardening gear. The gap between both is straightforward: A spade is created for grinding, and a spade was created for scooping and projecting. Shovels traditionally have curved and pointed blades, whereas spades possess flat, right, nearly rotating blades. A fantastic spade is vital in any garden for distributing dirt, manure, or compost. A spade is crucial for trimming or breaking fresh ground. But many gardeners use spades for whatever from cutting dirt luggage to hammering in bets. Very good spades are rocky. The two spades and shovels arrive in brief - and - long-handled versions. An extended handle gives you more leverage when digging holes, so bear this in mind if you are buying a new spade.

Garden Forks

As useful as a spade is for turning new garden dirt, I find an iron fork is a much better instrument for turning beds which were worked before. The fork can slip into the ground as deep as 12 inches, and at precisely the exact same time divides clods and loosens and aerates the soil greater than a shovel. Iron forks look very similar to short-handled spades except they have three to four iron tines in their own heads. The top ones will be those forged from 1 piece of steel with wood grips firmly attached. They are great not just for turning dirt but also for turning compost piles and smelling root crops, like carrots and potatoes.

Garden Rakes

When you dig soil, you have to level it, split dirt clods, and eloquent that the seedbeds (particularly if you're climbing beds that are raised). An iron rake is an ideal tool for the job though you can use it for this purpose just a few times annually. A 14-inch-diameter, iron-toothed rake ought to have a long, wooden handle that is securely attached to a metallic head. You may turn the metallic head to actually smooth a seedbed level. To get a lightweight but less lasting version of an iron rake, then try out an aluminum rake.

Buckets, Wagons, also Baskets

You do not possess a 1,000-square-foot garden. However, you still should carry seeds, fertilizer, tools, create, and other things around. I enjoy speaking about storage containers since this is where the tools of this trade get very straightforward. Listed below are 3 fundamental containers:

✓ **Buckets:** For potting soil, fertilizers, and hand tools, a 5-gallon plastic bucket is the best container. You are likely to get one free in the building site simply be certain that you wash it out nicely. To get a more durable but smaller bucket, then purchase one made out of galvanized steel.

✓ **Wagons:** For lighter things, like apartments of seedlings, use a kid's old red wagon. Wagons are fantastic for transferring plants and tiny bags of compost in your garden, along with the lip to the wagon bed helps maintain these things in place when you pay bumpy ground. If you are considering a wagon to maneuver yourself (rather than just gear) around the garden, you can utilize a type of wagon which is a saddle using a chair. This sort of wagon generally has a swiveling chair and can be perched on four analog wheels, letting you sit down and push yourself throughout the garden as you operate. Its storage space under the chair too.

✓ **Baskets:** To collect that entire fantastic make you develop and harvest, put money into a cable or wicker basket. Wire baskets are easier to use as it is possible to wash the produce while it's still from the basket. Wicker and wooden baskets, even though more durable than steel, are more aesthetically pleasing and trendy in your garden. Piling your vegetables in a basket is much more functional than attempting to balance zucchinis on your arms while taking them out of the garden to your kitchen.

Chapter 2: What Is The Best Soil?

Soil

A rich calcium source, gypsum is essential for keeping your soil light and fluffy. It is especially useful for opening up heavy clay-based soils making them much easier to dig. Many gardeners ignore gypsum thinking that it is just used to break up clay soils, but gypsum also adds two important nutrients to your garden - calcium and Sulphur. Calcium is beneficial to the soil just as Sulphur. As a matter of fact, if you were to place all the nutrients in order of importance for plant health, Sulphur would be 9th and calcium 7th.

One of the key benefits of Sulphur is its ability to regulate the sodium in the soil. If your soil has too much sodium then the calcium becomes unavailable to your plants - no matter how much calcium you add to your soil!

Unlike agricultural and dolomite limes which do not dissolve into the soil and must be dug in to have any effect, the calcium in gypsum is water-soluble and immediately available to plant roots.

Gypsum loosens up compacted soils is because the Sulphur leeches excess sodium from the soil and replaces it with calcium. Plant roots are slower to grow in compacted soils, not because of the smaller pore space, but because compacted soils have too much sodium and excess sodium burns and discourage root development.

Gypsum also helps organic matter and nutrients move through soils, which is why gypsum-treated soils have deeper topsoil than soils where no gypsum has been applied. In short, if you want to create well-balanced deep black soils then you need to apply gypsum to your garden beds regularly.

Types of Soil

Clay Soil

This type of soil feels lumpy and may feel sticky too when wet and it is rock-hard when it is dry. Clay soils drain poorly and it has fewer air spaces. This type of soil is heavy to cultivate but if drainage is improved well, plants grow better because clay soil holds a lot of nutrients than any other soil.

Sandy Soil

This type of soil is free-draining soil and is gritty when you touch it. Unlike clay soil, sandy soil warms quickly in the spring season. It is easier to cultivate but this type of soil may lack out nutrients because nutrients are easily washed through the soil in wet weather.

Silty Soil

The Silty soil is smooth and soapy when you touch it. This is a well-drained soil and is richer in nutrients than sandy soil because Silty Soils have more fertile soil. The soil structure is weak but it is a very good soil if it is managed well.

Peaty Soil

This type of soil contains a much higher level of peat or proportion of organic matter because of the soil's acidic nature which inhibits decomposition. But even though this contains higher peat, this soil has fewer nutrients. It is dark in color and it warms up quickly in spring.

Chalky Soil

The chalky soil is alkaline with a pH level of 7.5 or more. This type of stone is usually stony and has free draining. This type of soil can be remedied by using fertilizers which will make minerals like Manganese and Iron available to the plants making the plants avoid the yellowing of the seeds.

Loamy Soil

The loamy soil is known as the perfect soil for gardening. This has a good structure and it drains well too. This also retains moisture and is also full of nutrients! This type of soil is easy to cultivate and it warms up quickly in spring but it does not dry out when it is summer. You can consider yourself a lucky gardener if you have this type of soil!

Fertilizing

Nitrogen, Potassium, and Phosphorus amounts vary greatly depending on the different seeds being used in the meal. Generally, seed meals with high protein content will have equally high concentrations of NPK, whereas low protein seeds will have lower NPK values. Here are the most common seed meals with their protein and NPK ratios:

- Neem - 34% protein with an NPK of 6-1-2 (my preferred seed meal)

- Alfalfa - 17% with 2-1-2

- Soy - 36% with 7-2-1

- Cotton - 33% with 5-2-1

You can find many different seed meals for cheap prices at livestock and farm supply stores, where they are sold as a livestock feed replacement. Seed meals are popular among farmers because the high carbohydrate content can quickly fatten an animal in the final weeks before they send it to slaughter.

Protecting Your Plants with Lime

Regularly adding lime to your garden soils is easily the single most important thing you can do to grow better vegetables. Adding lime to your soil will help your plants grow big and strong. Calcium, which is the main component in most limes, will ensure your plants grow strong cell walls, enabling them to fight off pests and diseases easily.

Even if your garden soil is alkaline, the addition of a small amount of lime in this fertilizer will not increase the pH of your soil, unless it is below 6.0. The pH scale is not a linear measurement from 1-14 like many people think, instead it is a logarithmic scale where each number is 10 times greater than the last.

Increasing your soil's pH with the addition of lime is easy in acidic soils that have a pH of less than 6.0, but the higher the pH the less effect lime has on the soil. High pH soils generally have a high level of calcium, but this calcium is locked up in unavailable forms which is why you still need to apply lime to even alkaline soils.

If you plan to use a chicken tractor or spreading compost over your beds then this will tend to make your soil more acidic over time. Vegetables like to grow in soils with a pH between 6 and 6.5, anything below 5 or above 7 tends to reduce the growth and yields of most vegetable crops.

Benefit Of Composting

The many benefits of compost include:

1. It Makes Plants Healthier

Expert gardeners call compost "black gold" for a reason. It is the single most effective thing that you can do to improve the quality of your soil. And high-quality, fertile soil makes all the difference when you are trying to grow something -- whether it is grass, trees, shrubs, flowers, fruits, or vegetables. Compost is alive -- it adds beneficial microbes and nutrients to your soil. Healthy soil results in more significant, more robust plants that fight off disease and flourish even in less-than-optimal conditions.

2. It's Good for the Environment

According to a study made by the Environmental Protection Agency, yard trimmings and food scraps make up 23 percent of the total garbage in the United States. In 2000, 56.9 percent of those materials were composted. (Which is significant progress, because only

12 percent of those materials were composted ten years earlier, in 1990.) But that still means 43.1 percent of yard trimmings and food scraps go straight to the landfill, where they are entirely wasted. Landfill space is limited, and it costs money to put something there. Why throw stuff away at a great expense when we can turn it into rich compost instead? We must be responsible rather than dumping all our compostable materials into a landfill.

3. It Saves You Money

Making your own compost can reduce or eliminate the money you would otherwise spend to buy it from your local garden supply center. And compost that you make yourself is often better quality. Bagged compost is usually made from just one bulk material, like cow manure or cotton burrs. Compost that is made from a mix of yard and garden waste and food scraps has a wider variety of nutrients, which makes it richer and better for your soil.

Making your own compost saves money in other ways too. Plants growing in rich, healthy soil are naturally healthier, and not as susceptible to pests and plant diseases. This means you will spend less time and money on pest and disease control measures. And you will spend less money replacing plants that have died.

4. It Optimizes Soil Drainage

Do you have sandy soil that needs a lot of water to keep your plants happy? If so, then finished compost will act like a sponge, slowing down the drainage and keeping more water available for your plants. This means watering less often! Composted soil is also more resistant to erosion -- poor-quality soil washes away quickly when it is flooded, but rich soil is able to absorb water and release it later.

5. It Balances and Buffers Your Soil pH

You've probably read how most plants do best with a soil pH near neutral (7). Soil that is too acidic or too alkaline can prevent plant roots from absorbing essential nutrients. What happens when you add compost? The complex organic matter in compost helps to balance your soil and bring it closer to neutral, raising the pH of acidic soil and lowering the pH of alkaline soil. Compost also has the ability to absorb acid or alkaline additions to your soil, thus buffering your soil from sudden pH swings.

Types Of Composting

Backyard Or Onsite Composting

Homeowners, small businesses, and backyard garden enthusiasts can reduce their organic disposal costs by onsite composting. Yard trimmings and a wide variety of fresh food scraps can be composted right on the property. Commercial establishments and large institutions such as hospitals, universities, and prisons that generate huge quantities of food scraps may compost in situ if their campuses are big enough to allocate the space needed. When lawns are mowed regularly, the grass clippings can be left on the lawn to decompose naturally. This is known as grasscycling – the grass cuttings decay and enrich the turf. Onsite composters may rake up leaves into piles, and leave them to use later as mulch.

Very little time or equipment is required for backyard or onsite composting. Local residents may wish to educate one another by sharing composting tips and techniques. Or they can organize composting demonstrations and seminars to educate and encourage their neighbors or businesses in their community to compost on their own properties. Converting organic material to compost may take as long as two years. Manual turning can accelerate the decomposition significantly to less than 6 months or less.

Compost Tea

Beneficial microbes are extracted from vermicomposting and other types of high-density microbial compost. Compost tea is made by steeping or soaking compost in water for three days to a week. Water, air, food, and comfort are the four essentials for microbes to flourish. The water used for compost tea must be clean and de-chlorinated. Pure drinking (potable) water is perfect. Air is mixed into the "brewing" by a system of pipes that delivers oxygen to the microbes. Packaged nutrient mixes are added to the liquid to feed the colonies of fungi and bacteria.

The "brewed" tea is sprayed on seedlings, on the non-edible parts of vegetation or it is worked into the soil as a drench to treat root tips. The microbes get down to work to suppress disease and help the soil retain moisture and nutrients. Compost tea controls some fungal plant diseases on plant leaves so it can replace some toxic garden pesticides and fungicides.

Leaf-Mold Tea Or Green Manure Tea

Some leguminous plants like beans, peanuts, soybeans, and other perennials are rich in nitrogen. A nutritious "tea" is made from the leaves of such plants. Many crop leaves and wild greens such as comfrey and tithonia (wild sunflower species) may also be used to make leaf-mold tea. To make leaf-mold tea, a small pile of shredded or mashed-up leaves is wrapped in cheesecloth, burlap, or any suitable material, including nylon netting. The packet is immersed in a large bucket of water. If the leaf packet threatens to float, it is weighed down with a rock or some bricks. It is left for three days or longer to steep or to brew. The "teabag" is unwrapped and the contents are dumped into the compost heap. Leaf-mold or green manure tea is splashed directly on plants. This tea is mild so it doesn't burn young plants, even seedlings.

Vermicomposting

Vermicomposting uses worms to break down organic matter in compost bins. Ordinary earthworms in the garden could be used (if you have the patience to dig them up and transfer them into the bin). A variety of worm species including earthworms, white worms, and red wigglers are used to produce vermicast. The worm poop, called castings, is high-value compost. This high-quality end-product is also known as worm manure, worm castings, and worm humus. (Paper on Invasive Worms)

Vermiculture experts prefer red wigglers because they are voracious eaters and they breed fast. Compared to conventional composting, vermicomposting produces compost quicker as worms convert organic matter to usable end-product faster. When earthworms digest their food, they mix up minerals and nutrients into simple forms that are easy for plants to absorb. Beneficial microbes in the worms' digestive tract help to efficiently break down food particles that eventually enrich the soil. Vermicast is less saline so it can be applied directly to plants without risking "burning" sensitive plant parts. (Lazcano, Gomez-Brandon and Dominguez 2008)

In-vessel Composting

This large-scale operation requires expensive concrete-lined trenches, silos, sturdy drums, and similar equipment to contain the organic matter to be composted. Aeration, moisture, and temperature are vigilantly monitored, often electronically. Unlike the weather constraints of windrow and static pile composting, in-vessel composting can be done in all and even extreme climatic conditions with proper insulation.

A mechanism in the composting vessel turns or agitates the organic matter to aerate it properly. Large volumes of any organic waste including biosolids, animal manure, food scraps, and meat or other animal byproducts can be accommodated in in-vessel composters. The vessels vary in size, some as large as a school bus and others small enough to fit into a restaurant or school kitchen.

Grub Composting

This is a very fast technique for making compost. Black soldier flies are kept in "cages" where they lay their eggs. The eggs hatch into larvae or grubs. Enthusiasts and breeders say grub composting can be done in the garage, the bedroom, and even the kitchen because the bins are sanitary and the whole operation is basically odorless and tidy. Grubs quickly convert kitchen waste and animal manure into usable compost. Grubs are at least 50 times more efficient than earthworms and other wigglers at composting waste.

It could be fascinating to watch masses of these creepy crawlies devour huge quantities of organic waste such as fruit peel and food scraps, meat, and even animal manure. Chopping and shredding would not be necessary. The voracious grubs are incredible eating machines - they consume almost everything, including rotting vegetation dumped into the bins. The sawdust-like and odorless grub poop is called fry, a useful compost residue. Earthworms love grub poop.

Cockroach Composting

Yes, cockroaches are amazingly efficient composters. Cockroaches can eat anything and everything, they reproduce like crazy, need only super-low maintenance, and don't smell. Cockroaches are difficult to kill except by using disastrous chemicals. You may find it disgusting to think of raising cockroaches to do composting, but, it's true, these hardy insects can convert kitchen waste and even manure into compost much faster than the traditional compost heap.

Species such as the Turkestan cockroach or Blaptica dubia, Blatta lateralis, and others are used. While cockroaches produce fewer droppings than other invertebrates used for composting, the castings are more nutrient-dense. At different stages, cockroaches molt, and the chitin from the molts boosts the quality of the compost. Excess insects can be fed to farm animals and pets like bearded dragons, geckos, and some birds.

Cockroach composting is unconventional, weird, and freaky. One has to overcome the initial disgust of cockroaches. But, the efficiency of these disgusting insects makes up for the prejudice targeted at them. A discarded aquarium tank or any large-enough container can be used as cockroach bins. All kinds of food can be tossed into the cockroach breeding pen - nasty moldy food, dog food, people food - all leftovers. Prolific breeders, a cockroach colony can grow at astonishing speed. Each capsule-looking egg case contains 20 to 30 eggs.

Aerated (turned) windrow composting

"Windrows" are long piles of organic waste laid out in the field. These long rows, 14 to 16 feet wide, are turned manually or mechanically from time to time to aerate them. Windrows need to be between 4 and 8 feet high for them to be sufficiently hot and still allow oxygen to reach the core. Aerated windrow composting accommodates huge quantities of organic wastes such as those generated by sizeable communities and businesses that process high volumes of food such as packing plants, restaurants, and cafeterias.

Diverse wastes such as yard trimmings, animal byproducts, grease, liquids, or slurry are incorporated in windrows that are turned frequently and carefully monitored by municipal environment agencies. Sturdy equipment and labor are needed. In cold climates, the outside portions of windrows may freeze but the core can maintain 140° F. To retain the moisture in windrows, shelters are sometimes built over the whole lengths of the windows.

During the rainy seasons, the piles are adjusted to allow water to drain off instead of seeping into the heap. Aerated windrow composting is a large-scale operation that requires proper environmental measures to address issues such as leachate that might contaminate ground and surface-water supplies, control of odors and pest infestation, community zoning, and other public health concerns. Windrow composting yields huge amounts of compost that some local governments give for free or very little cost to encourage more residents to do organic gardening.

Chapter 3: The "Lasagna" Method

Firstly, to clear up any confusion, Lasagna Gardening is known by a number of names including Layer Composting, Layer gardening, Sheet Composting, or Lasagna Composting. Call it what you like but it all adds up to the same thing.

Easy weed-free, no-till gardening, that uses up as much organic waste as you can provide, that will, in turn, produce an abundance of crops at very little expense in both materials and labor.

It can be used alongside or in conjunction with other small gardening ideas, such as Raised Bed Gardening or Container Gardening. And it can be used in any area of the garden that gets sufficient sunshine for plants to grow.

Although some would claim it is a new idea, it is in essence a modern twist on an ancient concept and has in fact been used under different names or descriptions since ancient times.

However, the title 'Lasagna Gardening' alongside the others mentioned are indeed the product of the late 19th century till now.

In essence, a Lasagna garden is a layered rubbish heap filled with organic material, either by accident or design. The ancient Scots for instance referred to this as a Midden. A place where all food waste and animal dung would be dumped.

It was most likely realized that some of the waste vegetables took root and thrived in these conditions, and soon the Midden itself was used to grow vegetable crops.

I myself have known of this method since I was a child, as my parents were both crofters in a remote area of Northern Scotland, near Montrose.

Of course, things have changed a lot since then, and the concept of growing healthy organic vegetables in a rubbish heap has 'evolved' into the Lasagna Gardening style (amongst others) as we now know it.

Advantages Of A Lasagna Veggie Garden

1: Excellent Re-cycling: This is a great way to convert any old organic waste into fresh vegetables! Old newspaper, cardboard boxes, kitchen waste, etc. These can all be gathered and used to build up your Lasagna vegetable garden.

2: No Digging Required: This is a classic form of no-till gardening. The materials are simply thrown onto a layered heap, and the seedling or seeds planted in the pile.

The material does not get turned over at all, and the only digging required is the actual act of digging a small hole to plant your seedlings.

3: No Weeding: At least for the first few months of use, the Lasagna garden does not require weeding. This is mainly due to the fact that you are using a 'clean' growing medium, instead of weed-seed infested topsoil.

Some weeds will eventually make their way onto your Lasagna garden heap, but these are easily pulled up from the soft composting material.

4: No Fertilizers required: As the layered heap decomposes it creates a nutrient-rich growing medium. This means that you save money and effort as the plants have all the nutrients they need to thrive.

It also means that you can grow 100% organic, chemical-free vegetables for the family!

5: An excellent use of non-productive land: If you are 'blessed' with hard Stoney or otherwise poor soil on which to grow anything, then this method could be just what you are looking for!

The layered garden can be laid out on any piece of ground – even concrete! Just mark out your area (more on this later) and pile on your materials to create a super-productive vegetable bed.

I could go on – but I'm sure you get the idea by now!

Building A Lasagna Garden

Now we get down to the 'nuts & bolts' of Lasagna gardening, and in particular how to go about the construction itself.

Step 1: Find a suitable position: As mentioned earlier, you do not need to worry about the suitability of the ground with regard to growing your vegetables. This means that *with regard to the actual growing* of the vegetables, there are really only two main criteria to satisfy, and they are water supply and natural daylight.

Of course, depending on your situation you may have to consider predation by rabbits, deer, or other critters that love to munch on fresh vegetables. You may even have to consider possible vandalism or theft.

With regards to the actual plants' needs though, sun, water, and nutrients are the main considerations. The nutrients are already taken care of as the heap decomposes, with perhaps the possibility of a 'top-up' with organic fertilizer or tea.

Make sure that you are near to a water supply, as it can be a real drag if you are having to manhandle gallons of water to keep your veggies from expiring!

Most vegetables need a minimum of 8 hours of sunlight to grow, so be sure to pick a suitable spot in the yard that is not too shaded to suit your particular choice of vegetables.

Also, you should avoid setting up your Lasagna garden under over-hanging branches or heavy dense foliage. This will not only take sunshine away from your plants but can also lead to disease or insect infestation (especially aphids) amongst your vegetables.

Step 2: Collect your materials: What should you include in your Lasagna garden? Basically, everything that you put into your compost heap can be put into a Lasagna garden.

This is a shortlist of materials that *should be* included in a compost pile or indeed lasagna garden.

Carbon (Dried Matter): Dried leaves, straw, wood chips, sawdust, dried grass, straw, cardboard, paper (not colored), small twigs.

Nitrogen (Green matter): Fruit & Vegetable scraps, lawn clippings, weeds, plant cuttings, animal manure (herbivores only), old flowers.

Materials *NOT to include* in your compost for a variety of reasons include...

Anything inorganic such as plastic, polythene, polystyrene, etc. This should be a no-brainer as neither of these things decomposes – but it has to be said :)

Pet Poop: Dog or cat droppings should NEVER be added to the compost heap, as this can add several disease organisms as well as larvae to the mix.

Fat, fish, meat, bones, and dairy products: Should definitely not be added as they will attract rats and mice. They will also putrefy rather than decompose, which will cause your compost to smell bad.

Coal ash: The ashes from coal contain large amounts of Sulfur which is bad news for most plants, however, timber ash contains potash which is good especially for fruiting plants.

Colored paper: The paper from glossy magazines or any other colored paper should not be included, as the colors contain many harmful or toxic chemicals.

Diseased plants: Never add diseased plants to the layers as they are likely to spread the disease to your new vegetables. Dispose of them by burning if possible.

Once you have gathered together a suitable quantity of material to form your Lasagna garden – it should preferably be enough to form a heap 18-24 inches deep – then it is time to layer it up.

Step 3: Assembling the materials: Once you have the materials assembled you should roughly sort them into two categories: browns and greens.

The way it all works is this. The 'brown' material allows for ventilation or aeration of the heap as well as adding carbon. The 'green' material adds all the needed nutrients such as nitrogen & potassium.

The more 'green' material you have, then the faster the heap will decompose, and indeed the hotter it will get in the process. This is the basic premise behind Hot Bed Gardening – an early-season gardening method.

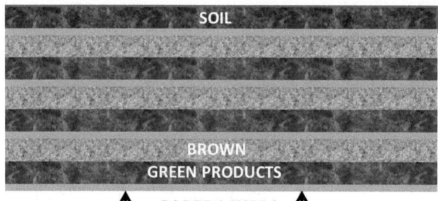

To make the Lasagna garden, I opt for a mix of approximately 3-4 parts 'brown' material to 1 part 'green.' This allows for a longer composting process and produces good results throughout the growing season.

The diagram below gives an example of a layered composting system. Whilst this looks nice and tidy in the diagram, the reality is that your Lasagna garden can look like a dog's breakfast – but not to worry :)

The layer of soil in the above diagram is optional, as shall be explained in the following part.

Grey Color = Paper or cardboard material (avoid glossy mags or rich colors).

Green = Organic nitrogen-rich vegetation such as grass cuttings, kitchen waste, manure, fruit, etc.

Light Brown = Carbon material such as wood shavings, sawdust, small twigs/branches, shredded newspaper.

Dark Brown = A 3-inch layer of compost or soil.

To set up the Lasagna system, start by laying out a few sheets of newspaper (5-10) or a layer of cardboard, and soak them thoroughly.

This can be laid directly over grass, weeds, whatever, as the paper/cardboard will stop the growth in its tracks.

I did mention earlier that you can even do this on top of concrete? This is true as you are not dependent on the surrounding soil in any way for your garden to operate. However, building it on concrete does lose the advantage of the natural process, where microbes and worms in *the* soil would help greatly in the composting process.

Yes, it will still function ok as nature gets to work, but for best results, it is better situated on soil or even a gravel bed.

On top of this layer of paper, pile a thick layer of brown material then your green material, then add to this your brown material. This is in turn topped by more paper or cardboard.

Repeat this process (watering throughout) until you have a layered bed at least 18 inches deep. Top-off the bed with a final layer of paper or cardboard.

Alternatively, if you want to begin growing vegetables immediately, top off the heap with 2-3 inches of good topsoil or better still a good growing medium such as a compost/peat/sand mix at 1/3rd each.

What now?

At this point there are a couple of choices open to you, depending on your particular circumstances.

If it happens to be the beginning of the growing season for you, then you can actually begin planting immediately by either topping off the pile with top-soil as previously described. Or alternatively, just dig a small pot-sized hole in the top layer and fill it with soil to get your plants started.

If it is later in the season and you need to leave it for a few months before starting, then you can either just walk away and let the whole mix rot-down; or you can cover it over with a tarp and leave it till spring. This will speed up the decomposition process and allow the worms and microbes to do their thing undisturbed.

Remove the tarp in the spring and plant your veggies!

Bear in mind that as the heap decomposes, the level will drop significantly over the ensuing weeks/months. This is to be expected and is merely a sign that the composting process is going as hoped.

Bit of a mess? Well yes, it can look a bit of an untidy mess, however, there are at least 3 simple solutions if you like your veggie plot to be nice and neat – and you don't mind a little extra work.

The first method is to simply create a wooden frame or box exactly the same as you would for a Raised Bed garden, and fill it in with the Lasagna composting method as described.

In the picture above you can see an example of a Raised Bed that is 2 feet high – which makes it easy on the 'old back,' since there is not a lot of bending over needed!

This box can be made using numerous different materials, anything that will contain the 'mess' within will do fine. Even chicken mesh can be used effectively to contain the infill. In fact, this method helps in the composting process as it allows air into the heap.

The Raised Bed example above is admittedly large; however, you can build it to any size that suits your needs – or material supply!

Another method which is perhaps more physical work but is less expensive to do is the 'trench style' Lasagna garden.

This involves digging out a hole or trench to the dimensions needed. Infill the organic material in exactly the same way as described earlier until it is 4 inches or so from the surface ground level.

Finish off by adding topsoil or growing mix until it is 2-3 inches proud of the surrounding ground level. This will compensate to some extent the sinking effect as decomposition takes place. At the end of the season, the pit can be topped up again to level it up with the rest of the veggie plot.

Yet another way, is in fact a combination of the first 2 methods. Instead of digging a pit 18-24 inches deep – which can involve some serious hard work, split the difference by digging a shallow pit only 6-12 inches deep and surround with a wooden frame to make up the difference.

For instance, a pit dug at 6 inches deep will need a 12-18 inches frame on top of the pit to make up a minimum of 18 inches of composting material.

The diagram above provides an example of a semi-sunken pit for Lasagna gardening. As an addition to this especially if you have water-logged or boggy ground, you could consider digging a sump at the bottom of the pit and filling it with loose stones or crushed gravel to act as a drain.

The bottom line is that there is little you can do 'wrong' when building your Lasagna garden. Just get a good mix of brown and green materials together and pile them up in an approximation of the manner described, and you will have a nutrient-rich bed in which to grow your veggies.

This method is also applicable to containers of many shapes and sizes, providing the container is large enough to infill with multiple layers of organic materials.

Planting Guide

So, what exactly can you grow in a layered garden? The answer to this is easy – virtually anything that can be grown in a traditional garden!

Ok, so this is somewhat dependent on how you go about planting your veggies, to begin with.

For instance, if you are planting straight into the top of the heap with no covering of soil, then I would not try growing deep-rooted plants such as carrots or parsnips – at least not until the heap has had several months to break down.

The reason for this is that the roots will immediately hit obstructions from the cardboard or other brown material. This will result in the root going off in different directions, in much the same way as it would if you planted it in Stoney soil. See the pic below...

I'm fairly sure you will agree that this is not a good look :) It is however easily avoided by either waiting for a few months (build it late autumn and plant it out in the spring) for the material to break down thereby allowing the roots 'safe passage' or by using the following method.

With a garden knife or sharp spade, cut down into the top of the heap at least 6 inches then move the spade from side to side so that a 'V' shaped channel is formed in the heap.

Fill this in with a good compost mix before sprinkling a thin row of seeds along with it. This will create a perfect environment for your carrots to grow in and should result in healthy, straight roots.

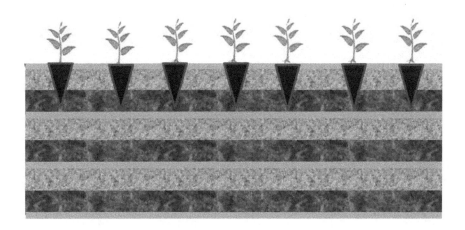

This is exactly the same method as you would use when growing carrots or parsnips in a Straw Bale vegetable garden, and it is extremely effective.

There are of course many hundreds of different vegetables you can grow yourself, depending on factors such as your location, growing outside or in a hothouse, or indeed what you personally like or prefer to grow.

Written as a general guide to planting vegetables in a 'normal' garden set-up, it should be noted that vegetables grown in a Lasagna garden can be planted closer together than usual. This is due to several factors as listed below.

1. The growing medium is nutrient-rich; therefore, the plants are not fighting other plants for nutrients.
2. The fact that weeds are not so much of a problem in this gardening technique, means that you do not need to allow space for a garden hoe to get through.
3. As in point 1- The fact is that the veggies are not competing with weeds for nutrients and water.

Chapter 4: Easy To Grow Plants For Beginners

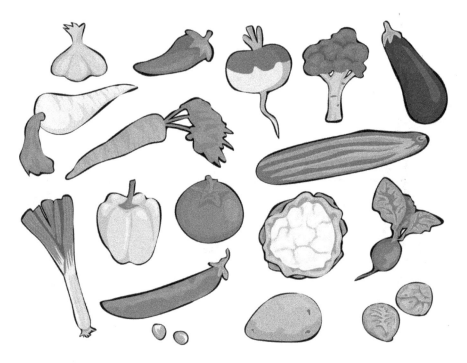

Warm Season and Cool Season Vegetables

You'll find information on plant families, feeding characteristics, and what pest and pathogen problems may affect each species. The plants are listed alphabetically, and this information should help you decide what vegetables you want to grow in your garden.

You can grow your own rainbow of crops!

Beans

- warm-season crop of the legume family
- light feeder, returns nitrogen to the soil
- pests: beetles, slugs, whiteflies, and cutworms
- pathogens: powdery mildew, white mold, mosaic virus
- sowing: direct sow after the threat of frost has passed
- planting: place seeds 1" deep, 2"-3" apart, rows separated by 18"
- harvest: pick when beans are as thick as a pencil
- storage: eat fresh within a week; freeze or can long-term
- quick info: the more you harvest, the more they'll produce

Beets

- cool-season crop of the beetroot family
- light feeder
- pests: leaf miners, leafhoppers, flea beetles
- pathogens: leaf spot, mosaic virus
- sowing: direct sow in early spring, once it hits 50 degrees

- planting: place seeds ½" deep, 2"-3" apart, rows separated by 12"
- harvest: best at 55-70 days, when roots are golf to tennis ball-size
- storage: eat fresh within a week; prepare and can, or dry store
- quick info: thin beet seedlings by snipping young greens for salads

Broccoli

- cool-season crop of the brassica family
- heavy feeder
- pests: aphids, cabbage worms, whiteflies
- pathogens: clubroot, white rust
- sowing: indoors in early spring, direct sow 3 weeks after last frost
- planting: place seeds ½" deep, 3" apart, rows no closer than 12"
- harvest: after 85 days, best picked in the morning
- storage: eat fresh within 5 days; prepare and freeze long-term
- quick info: keep the heads dry when watering to avoid rot

Brussels Sprouts

- cool-season crop of the brassica family
- heavy feeder
- pests: aphids, cabbage worms, whiteflies
- pathogens: clubroot, downy mildew, white mold
- sowing: indoors in early spring, direct sow 3 weeks after last frost
- planting: place seeds ½" deep, 2"-3" apart, rows no closer than 12"
- harvest: when globes are 1"-2" around
- storage: eat fresh within a week; freeze or can long-term
- quick info: encourage larger globes by trimming back top leaves

Cabbage

- cool-season crop of the brassica family
- heavy feeder
- pests: aphids, cabbage worms, loopers, cutworms, whiteflies
- pathogens: clubroot, downy mildew
- sowing: indoors in early spring, transplant when cloudy

- planting: carefully place seedlings no closer than 12"
- harvest: around 70 days, mature heads will begin to split
- storage: eat fresh within two weeks; dry storage for three months
- quick info: very heavy feeders- don't place them too close together

Carrots

- warm-season crop of the parsley family
- light feeder
- pests: carrot rust flies, flea beetles, wireworms
- pathogens: black canker, yellow aster disease (both rare)
- sowing: direct sow 3-5 weeks before last frost
- planting: place seeds ¼" deep, 2"-3" apart, in rows 12" apart
- harvest: when carrots are at least a half-inch thick
- storage: seal fresh carrots in airtight bags; freeze, can, or dry-store
- quick info: smaller=sweeter; carrots can withstand frost

Cauliflower

- cool-season crop of the brassica family
- heavy feeder
- pests: aphids, cabbage worms, whiteflies
- pathogens: clubroot, powdery mildew, white rust
- sowing: best results from nursery stock, plant before last frost
- planting: transplant 18-24" inches apart, in wide rows
- harvest: 80 days from transplant, when heads firm and tighten
- storage: eat fresh within a week; prepare and freeze long-term
- quick info: tie leaves up overhead a week before harvest to protect

Cucumbers

- warm-season crop of the cucurbit family
- medium feeder
- pests: aphids, cucumber beetles, squash bugs
- pathogens: blossom end rot, powdery mildew
- sowing: indoors, three weeks before transplant
- planting: when the soil reaches 70 degrees, 3" apart in narrow rows

- harvest: when fruits reach 2" (picklers) to 8" long (salad)
- storage: eat fresh within a week; pickle and can long-term
- quick info: harvest early and often to maximize each plant's output

Eggplant

- warm-season crop of the nightshade family
- medium feeder
- pests: flea beetles, hornworms
- pathogens: powdery mildew

- sowing: indoors in early spring, transplant 2 weeks after last frost
- planting: 2'-3' apart, in rows 3'-4' apart- need lots of space
- harvest: 65- 80 days after transplant, when fruits are firm/shiny
- storage: in the refrigerator for one week, take care not to break the skin
- quick info: stake or cage the plants when the fruit gets heavy

Kale

- cool-season crop of the brassica family
- light feeder
- pests: aphids, cabbage worms, flea beetles,
- pathogens: few known
- sowing: direct sow, 2-4 weeks before last frost
- planting: sow seeds ½" deep, thin young seedlings to 12" apart
- harvest: one 'fistful' at a time, do not harvest center bud
- storage: wash and refrigerate in a loose bag for one week

- quick info: eat raw or wilted, kale is rich in vitamins and minerals

Lettuce

- cool-season crop of the aster (daisy) family
- medium feeder
- pests: aphids, cutworms, earwigs, plus rabbits and woodchucks
- pathogens: white mold
- sowing: direct sow, after the weather is consistently over 40 degrees

- planting: sow seeds ½" deep, thin young seedlings to 12" apart
- harvest: Loose-leaf – cut outer leaves as wanted, or the whole head
  Crisp-head – when the head is firm, and leaves begin to peel
- storage: wash and refrigerate in a loose bag for one week
- quick info: lettuce will bolt and reseed itself if unharvested

Peas

- cool to early warm-season crop of the legume family
- light feeder, returns nitrogen to the soil
- pests: aphids, bean beetles, wireworms
- pathogens: downy mildew, fusarium wilt, powdery mildew
- sowing: direct sow, 4 weeks before last frost
- planting: place seeds 1" deep, 2" apart, in 2' wide rows
- harvest: 60-70 days, always harvest full stem to protect pods

- storage: eat fresh within a week; freeze, can, or dry pods long-term
- quick info: pea flowers are delicate, fragrant, and draw pollinators

Peppers

- warm-season crop of the nightshade family
- medium feeder
- pests: aphids, flea beetles, hornworms, potato beetles
- pathogens: anthracnose, blossom end rot, mosaic virus
- sowing: indoors in early spring, transplant 4 weeks after last frost
- planting: harden off before planting, space 18"-24" apart
- harvest: 80-100 days, the color will change the longer it remains on the plant
- storage: eat fresh within a week; freeze or dehydrate long-term
- quick info: the heat in a pepper comes from capsaicin in the seeds

Potatoes

- full season crop of the nightshade family
- medium feeder
- pests: aphids, flea beetles, potato beetles,
- pathogens: early or late blight, potato scab (pH imbalance)
- sowing: plant seed potatoes 4-6 weeks before last frost
- planting: place 3' apart, mound soil over roots as the plant grows
- harvest: 2-6 weeks after flowering, based on the desired size
- storage: eat fresh within 2 weeks; dry store long-term
- quick info: don't eat 'green' potatoes, they are mildly toxic

Pumpkins

- full season crop of the cucurbit family
- medium feeder
- pests: aphids, cucumber beetles, squash vine borers
- pathogens: anthracnose, powdery mildew

- sowing: direct sow, one month after last frost
- planting: place 4 seeds in a hill, with hills 12" apart, thin seedlings
- harvest: when full-size, deep in color, and hollow-sounding
- storage: use fresh for cooking; dry store long-term
- quick info: don't forget to roast the seeds; delicious and nutritious!

Radishes

- multi-harvest crop of the brassica family
- medium feeder
- pests: cabbage root maggots
- pathogens: clubroot
- sowing: direct sow in spring or fall
- planting: places seeds in a shallow trench, thin young seedlings
- harvest: 21-28 days, when roots are 1" round
- storage: eat fresh raw or cooked; freeze or dry store long-term
- quick info: radishes greens are also edible, raw, or pan-wilted

Spinach

- cool-season crop of the amaranth family
- heavy feeder
- pests: leaf miners
- pathogens: blight, downy mildew, mosaic virus
- sowing: direct sow immediately after last frost
- planting: place seeds in short rows, 12 seeds per 1", thin later
- harvest: when desired leaf size, either as needed or a whole head
- storage: wash and refrigerate in a loose bag for one week
- quick info: the larger the leaves, the more bitter the taste

Swiss Chard

- cool or warm-season crop of the beetroot family
- light feeder
- pests: aphids, leaf miners, slugs
- pathogens: leaf spot
- sowing: direct sow, 2-3 weeks before last frost
- planting: place seeds ½" deep, 2"-6" apart in narrow rows

- harvest: cut-as-you-go for chard all season, take outer leaves first
- storage: wash and refrigerate in a loose bag for one week
- quick info: plants over 1' tall will begin to lose flavor, harvest early

Sweet Potatoes

- full season crop of the bindweed (morning glory) family
- light to medium feeder
- pests: flea beetles
- pathogens: blight, leaf spot, scurf
- sowing: direct sow seed slips after the threat of frost has passed
- planting: place slips in 6" mounds, at least 12" apart
- harvest: after 100 days, or when the leaves and vines go yellow
- storage: eat fresh within days; cure well for long-term dry storage
- quick info: rich in Vitamin A; don't wash for better curing of skin

Tomatoes

- warm-season crop of the nightshade family
- heavy feeder
- pests: aphids, flea beetles, hornworms, whiteflies
- pathogens: blight, blossom end rot, mosaic virus
- sowing: indoors, in early spring
- planting: space seedlings no closer than 18", after last frost
- harvest: when fruit plumps and reddens, be gentle!
- storage: eat fresh within a week; process and can long-term
- quick info: stake or cage plants early to avoid damage

Winter Squash

- full season crop of the cucurbit family
- medium feeder
- pests: aphids, cucumber beetles, squash bugs, squash vine borer
- pathogens: blossom end rot, powdery mildew
- sowing: outdoors, 2-4 weeks after last frost, later for fall harvest

- planting: place 3-4 seeds in hills 6" apart, thin seedlings
- harvest: when fruits are medium-sized and firm
- storage: winter squash can be cured and stored for up to 3 months
- quick info: varieties include butternut, acorn, and spaghetti

Zucchini/Summer Squash

- warm-season crop of the cucurbit family
- medium feeder
- pests: aphids, cucumber beetles, squash bugs, squash vine borer
- pathogens: blossom end rot, powdery mildew
- sowing: outdoors, 2 weeks after last frost
- planting: place 3-4 seeds in hills 6" apart, thin seedlings
- harvest: when fruits are 10-12" long, larger will be pithy and bitter
- storage: eat fresh within a week; prepare and freeze long-term
- quick info: zucchini is prolific, bake lots of zucchini bread!

As you can see from this list, there are commonalities in the characteristics of plants in the same families. Being able to recognize their connections can help you be a better garden designer, diagnostician, and troubleshooter. Learning to grow the basic varieties of these vegetables will also give you the experience you need to branch out and try new cultivars and varieties, opening up a whole new world of fresh food for you to enjoy!

Herbs

Garlic

- Extra Easy, Container-Friendly, Raised Bed–Friendly
- Family: Amaryllidaceae
- Growing zones: N/A
- Growing season(s): cool weather
- Spacing: 6 to 8 inches
- Start indoors or direct sow: direct sow
- Indoor sowing date: N/A
- Earliest outdoor planting: 2 weeks before the average first frost
- Soil temperature: N/A

- Fall planting: N/A
- Sun needs: 6+ hours
- Water needs: low
- Harvest category: one harvest

Suggested varieties for beginners: soft-neck for warmer regions, hard-neck for cooler regions

Keep in Mind Tip: Although it's possible to plant garlic cloves you buy at the grocery store; I don't recommend it. First, this garlic is usually not certified disease-free, so you risk contaminating your garden soil for years to come. Second, you don't know whether that variety will grow in your region. Most garlic in grocery stores are soft-neck garlic, which grows well in the South but doesn't tolerate cold as well as hard-neck types.

Snapshot

Garlic is one of the easiest crops for a home gardener to grow. Planted in the fall for the following season, garlic requires little maintenance and is one of the first plants to begin growing in the early spring. An adaptable crop, garlic can be grown in the ground, in raised beds, and in containers.

Starting

Purchase certified disease-free bulbs of garlic from a reputable seed supplier. At around the time of your first fall frost, separate individual cloves from the bulb and plant pointy-side up in 2-inch-deep trenches. Cover with soil, and in cold-climate areas, spread an additional 1 to 2 inches of mulch. Water well at planting.

Growing

Garlic will likely sprout in the fall, stop growing through the winter, and start growing again in the late winter. Water isn't necessary during this dormant period; begin consistent light irrigation in the spring if rainfall is scarce. Keep the area well weeded (mulch helps).

Harvesting and Storing

Southern gardeners may start harvesting garlic in mid-May; northern growers may not harvest until late July. In either case, watch for the lower half of the leaves to turn brown and die off. Use a trowel to dig around the bulb to loosen the soil. Pull out the bulbs and move them to a shaded, well-ventilated location (such as a garage). Lay the bulbs in single layers or hang them. Set a fan on them if you live in a humid location and let them "cure" for 2 to 4 weeks. Curing is complete when the necks of the bulbs completely dry out. Clip the bulbs from the dry foliage, trim the roots, and move them to a root cellar or pantry for storage. Save the biggest bulbs in a loosely closed brown paper bag for your next crop.

Common Problem

Garlic usually has few problems. Abnormally rainy springs can cause poor bulb development, as can planting the cloves too close together. If you live in a wet area, plant garlic in raised beds or containers.

Onions

- Container-Friendly, Raised Bed–Friendly
- Family: Amaryllidaceae
- Growing zones: N/A
- Growing season(s): cool weather
- Spacing: 6 inches
- Start indoors or direct sow: start indoors or purchase transplants or sets
- Indoor sowing date: 10 weeks before transplant (16 weeks before average last frost)

- Earliest outdoor planting: 6 weeks before average last frost
- Soil temperature: 50° to 95°
- Fall planting: N/A
- Sun needs: 6+ hours
- Water needs: moderate
- Harvest category: one harvest
- Suggested varieties for beginners: Ailsa Craig (long-day), Yellow Granex (short-day)

Keep in Mind Tip: If you want to eat "green onions" (scallions), you can harvest the leaves at any time. Just keep in mind that those leaves help nourish the developing bulb; the more leaves you remove, the smaller the bulb will be. Consider planting a crop just for scallions that you can harvest throughout the season.

Snapshot

Onions are one of the most commonly used vegetables for cooking. The key to growing good onions is to choose the correct seeds, sets, or transplants for your area. In order to harvest a large bulb, gardeners in the southern United States must grow short-day onions, and gardeners in the North must grow long-day ones.

Gardeners in the middle parts of the country can try either type or purchase "day-neutral" varieties.

Starting

Most beginning gardeners plant onions from transplants or sets. Transplants look like scallions from the grocery store; sets look like baby onion bulbs. Most sets are long-day onions, so if you live in the South, double-check the variety or your onions won't bulb. Plant onions in well-drained soil amended with plenty of organic matter. Transplants should be planted with the white part underground; bury sets just beneath the soil's surface.

Growing

Keep the area well weeded. In the early months of growth, rainfall will likely provide sufficient water, but during hotter times of year or periods of drought, ensure onions receive 1 to 2 inches of irrigation per week. After the soil has warmed, apply a layer of mulch to help with weed control and to conserve moisture.

Harvesting and Storing

Onions are ready to harvest when the tops have yellowed and fallen over. Dig out the bulbs, being careful not to stab them with the trowel. Transfer them to a shaded, well-ventilated location where you can lay them in single layers or hang them. Let them "cure" until the stems have dried out and no moisture remains in the stem when you clip off the foliage. Store in a cool area such as a root cellar or the bottom of your pantry.

Common Problem

If the onion plant sends out a tall flower stalk before it's ready to harvest, the plant has bolted and bulb production has stopped. Early bolting is typically caused by environmental stress such as extreme temperature fluctuations or water issues. Keep the area mulched to moderate soil temperature. Upon bolting, harvest the onion bulbs and use them before other onions, because they will not store well.

Basil

- Extra Easy, Quick, Container-Friendly, Raised Bed–Friendly
- Family: Lamiaceae
- Growing zones: N/A
- Growing season(s): warm weather
- Spacing: 12 inches
- Start indoors or direct sow: either, or purchase transplants
- Indoor sowing date: 4 weeks before average last frost
- Earliest outdoor planting: after last spring frost
- Soil temperature: 60° to 90°
- Fall planting: N/A

- Sun needs: 6+ hours
- Water needs: moderate
- Harvest category: all season
- Suggested varieties for beginners: sweet basil, cinnamon basil, Genovese

Preparation Tip: Turn extra basil into a simple pesto. Combine 20 to 30 basil leaves, ¼ cup of olive oil, 2 garlic cloves, ½ teaspoon of salt, ¼ teaspoon of pepper, 1 tablespoon of pine nuts, and 2 tablespoons of Parmesan cheese in a food processor or blender and blend to a paste. Serve over angel-hair pasta or make larger batches to freeze.

Snapshot

Possibly the most popular herb in the home garden, basil is beloved for its fragrant and tasty leaves. Enjoyed fresh in Italian dishes or made into basil pesto, no home garden should be without this summer delight.

Starting

Basil thrives in warm weather. It will die in a frost and suffer damage when nights dip below 50°. For this reason, wait to plant basil (seeds or transplants) until a week or more after your last frost. If direct sowing, scatter seeds on top of the soil and scrape them in with your fingers. Water well and keep moist until germination.

Growing

Keep basil consistently moist but not waterlogged. For an all-season harvest, keep the plant trimmed, starting at about 6 inches high so it will bush out. Trim the tips of the stems when the leaves start forming a tight cluster in the center. Without proper pruning, those clusters will bloom into flowers (and eventually seeds), and the quality of the remaining leaves will decline.

Harvesting and Storing

Harvest basil early and often, and use fresh leaves immediately. If you need to store the leaves, cut them with stems that are long enough to place them upright in a glass of water in the refrigerator.

Common Problem

Basil loves to flower and go to seed quickly. But pollinators and beneficial insects love those flowers. Get the best of both worlds by planting multiple plants, keeping one trimmed for fresh use, and letting the others flower. When the flower pods dry out, gather the seeds to save for next season.

Cilantro

- Quick, Container-Friendly, Raised Bed–Friendly
- Family: Apiaceae
- Growing zones: N/A
- Growing season(s): cool weather
- Spacing: 6 inches
- Start indoors or direct sow: direct sow
- Indoor sowing date: N/A
- Earliest outdoor planting: as soon as soil can be worked
- Soil temperature: 55° to 68°
- Fall planting: 4 to 6 weeks before the average first frost
- Sun needs: 6+ hours
- Water needs: moderate
- Harvest category: weather dependent
- Suggested varieties for beginners: Slo-bolt, Santo

Fun Fact: Does cilantro taste like soap to you? It's not just you. A certain percentage of the population has a genetic sensitivity to aldehydes in cilantro leaves, which makes them perceive the flavor as soapy.

Snapshot

A love-it-or-hate-it herb, cilantro is a staple in many gardens. Cilantro, unlike the foods it's usually paired with, hates hot weather, and prefers the cool temperatures of fall, winter, and spring.

Starting

Sow cilantro seeds directly into the garden about 2 inches apart, thinning to 6 inches apart. Cilantro likes well-drained soil enriched with compost. Plant several plants if you plan to freeze or preserve them.

Growing

If you live in a hotter climate, mulch the plants well and consider afternoon shade to keep soil temperatures as low as possible for as long as possible.

Harvesting and Storing

Start harvesting cilantro when it's 6 inches tall. When the plant starts to bolt and flower, leave it, and you can harvest the seeds as the spice coriander.

Common Problem

Cilantro bolts quickly in warm weather, so harvest it frequently while it's small. The leaves turn bitter when they become feathery and the center stalk starts growing tall. Sow succession plantings to keep a continuous supply, then let the bolted plants flower and go to seed. As the plants drop the seed they may continuously self-sow. If you grow cilantro in the fall, you may have a longer harvest window.

Mint

- Extra Easy, Quick, Container-Friendly
- Family: Lamiaceae
- Growing zones: N/A
- Growing season(s): perennial in zones 3 (some varieties) +
- Spacing: 12 to 18 inches
- Start indoors or direct sow: purchase transplants
- Indoor sowing date: N/A
- Earliest outdoor planting: early spring
- Soil temperature: N/A
- Fall planting: N/A
- Sun needs: 6+ hours

- Water needs: high
- Harvest category: all season
- Suggested varieties for beginners: peppermint, spearmint, chocolate mint, lemon balm

Fun Fact: Peppermint is a well-known tummy soother. Pinch off fresh leaves and steep them in hot water for 10 minutes. Add honey if desired. (Not recommended for young children.)

Snapshot

Mints of all kinds are a delight in the garden. Just make sure to plant them in a well-contained place, as the plants spread invasively. Containers are the best solution. Use mint in hot tea, summertime fruit salads, and in cold, refreshing mint water. Once you learn the variety of uses for homegrown mint, you'll be glad you added it to your garden.

Starting

Purchase potted mint from your local garden center and plant it in rich, moist soil. It requires more water than other herbs, so consider this when combining herbs in large pots or beds.

Growing

Besides keeping mint plants well-watered (especially during the heat of the summer), the best care you can provide is pruning. Cut the plants frequently to keep them producing tender new leaves.

Harvesting and Storing

Cut mint as needed for fresh use. If it becomes woody, cut back the entire plant to promote new growth (you can do this a few times throughout the season). Dry the cuttings in a dehydrator or hang them upside down in a dark, airy location. Strip the leaves and store them in clean jars.

Common Problem

If your mint plant stops growing and seems to show woody rather than tender growth, most likely it has outgrown its pot. Wait for mild weather (not high heat or winter cold) and take the entire plant out of the pot. Divide it with a sharp knife and replant one division in fresh soil. Plant the other division in a separate container (or give to a friend). Water it well.

Parsley

- Quick, Container-Friendly, Raised Bed–Friendly
- Family: Apiaceae
- Growing zones: N/A
- Growing season(s): cool-weather biennial
- Spacing: 10 inches
- Start indoors or direct sow: either, or purchase transplants
- Indoor sowing date: 4 weeks before transplant (6 weeks before average last frost)
- Earliest outdoor planting: 2 weeks before average last frost
- Soil temperature: 50° to 80°
- Fall planting: in the South, plant transplants 4 weeks before first frost
- Sun needs: 4+ hours
- Water needs: moderate
- Harvest category: all season, weather dependent in some areas
- Suggested varieties for beginners: Italian dark green, curly parsley

Fun Fact: Whether parsley bolts in the first year or completes its growing cycle in the second year, if left to flower and drop seed, it may self-sow, giving you a continuous supply.

Snapshot

Parsley is said to intensify other flavors. However, the flavor profile amplifies when you grow it yourself. Dried parsley and store-bought parsley simply do not compare to the homegrown herb. When parsley is established and grown under ideal conditions, you can expect to harvest it for well over a year, until its growth cycle causes it to flower and set seed in its second year.

Starting

Though you can sow parsley from seed, it can take a long time to germinate. Many first-time gardeners prefer to purchase transplants. Plant parsley in moist but well-drained soil with plenty of organic matter.

Growing

Keep plants evenly watered. In the hotter summers of the South, parsley benefits from afternoon shade, because high temperatures and water stress can cause it to bolt in the first year. Southern growers may find fall planting to be more successful and will be able to harvest leaves all winter.

Harvesting and Storing

Begin harvesting when the plant reaches 6 inches in height, and harvest as needed. Or, for a larger harvest for drying, cut the plant back to 1 to 2 inches above soil level, where it will regrow leaves. Parsley can be dried, but the flavor will weaken considerably.

Common Problem

When the plant produces a tall center stalk, it has bolted. The leaves can still be used, though the flavor might become bitter. To prevent parsley from bolting, mulch the plants well and keep them watered to limit stress, especially in the hot summer.

Rosemary

- Extra Easy, Quick, Container-Friendly, Raised Bed–Friendly
- Family: Lamiaceae
- Growing zones: N/A
- Growing season(s): perennial in zones 7+
- Spacing: 36 inches
- Start indoors or direct sow: purchase transplants
- Indoor sowing date: N/A

- Earliest outdoor planting: early spring
- Soil temperature: N/A
- Fall planting: N/A
- Sun needs: 4+ hours
- Water needs: low
- Harvest category: all season (zones 7+), weather dependent (zones 6-)
- Suggested varieties for beginners: N/A

Troubleshooting Tip: Rosemary may not survive outdoors where temperatures dip below 5°; gardeners in borderline zones may have success planting rosemary in a southern-exposure location or in the ground with heavy mulch. Northern gardeners can bring rosemary pots inside for the winter.

Snapshot

A beautifully fragrant shrub, rosemary is perfect for a container patio garden and mixes well with other herbs. Light, well-drained soil is best for the plant, and it tolerates drought. After a few years, rosemary will become tough and woody; plan to replace old plants every few years for the best-quality herb.

Starting

Purchase a potted transplant from a local garden center. Water it well at transplant and it shouldn't have any trouble getting established.

Growing

Rosemary grown in the ground rarely requires supplemental irrigation. Potted rosemary should be monitored occasionally to ensure the soil doesn't dry out completely.

Harvesting and Storing

Snip leaves as necessary for fresh use. To harvest for storage purposes, cut the stems a few inches above where they have become woody, but don't harvest more than one-third of the plant at a time. Hang the cuttings upside down in a dark, airy location. When they're dry, strip the leaves and store them in a clean jar.

Common Problem

If the leaves turn brown, the plant likely received too much water. To avoid this problem, cut down on watering or, if the plant is outside, move it to a sheltered location during rainy periods or mulch it to help moderate the moisture.

Sage

- Extra Easy, Quick, Container-Friendly, Raised Bed–Friendly
- Family: Lamiaceae
- Growing zones: N/A
- Growing season(s): perennial in zones 4 to 8
- Spacing: 18 inches
- Start indoors or direct sow: purchase transplants
- Indoor sowing date: N/A
- Earliest outdoor planting: early spring
- Soil temperature: N/A
- Fall planting: N/A
- Sun needs: 6+ hours
- Water needs: low
- Harvest category: all season
- Suggested varieties for beginners: culinary sage

Fun Fact: Sage can be grown indoors on a sunny windowsill, giving you a fresh supply of the herb all winter. Choose a compact variety and cut back any flowers that form.

Snapshot

Sage is most commonly known as the spice in Thanksgiving dressing, but it's also a staple in sausage, meatloaf, and pork dishes. In most zones, sage grows as a perennial. It may lose its leaves in the winter but will regrow in the spring. In areas that don't receive frost, sage may not grow year-round because of a lack of chilling time needed for new growth.

Starting

Purchase a potted sage plant at your local garden center and plant it in light, well-drained soil. Water it well at planting.

Growing

Sage prefers full sun, but it may need partial shade in areas with hot summers. After the first year, cut back the entire plant to half its size after new growth begins to appear. This will keep the plant in check and also encourage new tender growth.

Harvesting and Storing

Pick sage leaves as needed for fresh use. Sage leaves can also be dried when cut back in the second year and ground into a spice.

Common Problem

Once established, sage prefers not to have a lot of water. If the soil is too heavy and rainfall causes it to stay saturated, it can show signs of disease. If you have a heavier soil, add sand or perlite to help with drainage.

Thyme

- Extra Easy, Quick, Container-Friendly, Raised Bed-Friendly
- Family: Lamiaceae
- Growing zones: N/A
- Growing season(s): perennial in zones 4+
- Spacing: 12 inches
- Start indoors or direct sow: purchase transplants
- Indoor sowing date: N/A
- Earliest outdoor planting: early spring
- Soil temperature: N/A
- Fall planting: N/A

- Sun needs: 4+ hours
- Water needs: low
- Harvest category: all season
- Suggested varieties for beginners: common thyme, English thyme, creeping thyme

Keep in Mind Tip: Because thyme will make its home in most gardens for several years, choose its location carefully.

Snapshot

A fuss-free, low-growing herb, thyme can grow in a trailing fashion or like a shrub. In zones 4 and above, thyme is a hardy perennial, and you can harvest from an established plant year-round.

Starting

Purchase potted thyme from your local nursery. Plant in well-draining soil; a container is a perfect choice.

Growing

Besides the initial watering, thyme requires little extra care. If you live in zone 4, mulch the plants before winter to protect them from the cold. Thyme doesn't like too much moisture, so mulch with fine gravel or pine needles instead of wood mulch.

Harvesting and Storing

Thyme can be harvested for fresh eating year-round for most gardeners. But if you want to dry larger quantities, cut back the entire plant just before it flowers, leaving 3 to 4 inches of growth at the bottom. The plant will regrow. Hang the sprigs upside down in a dark but ventilated room. Strip the leaves when they are dry and place them in a clean jar for storage.

Common Problem

After a few years, a thyme plant will become woody and the quality of the leaves will decline. Plan to replace your thyme plant every few years for a steady supply of high-quality, fragrant leaves.

Chapter 5: Common Problems and How to Avoid Them

Some people are gifted in gardening. For the rest of us, it takes a little learning and patience to develop intuitive gardening skills. Thankfully, indoor gardening is quite forgiving if you are attentive and notice problems that are beginning with your plants before they have the opportunity to grow into significant issues. We all know that there are problems common in outdoor gardens. Some of the potential problems with indoor gardens are slightly different. While outside growing conditions are certainly never perfect, much of the time, the conditions can correct themselves naturally or with a gentle human nudge. With indoor gardening, we need to recreate what occurs naturally outside of our walls and produce an environment in which plants can thrive. Below is the list of the most usually encountered problems with indoor kitchen gardens and what you can do to solve them and turn a potential gardening disaster into a success.

Abiotic Problems

Abiotic refers to the condition of the environment surrounding the plant, such as the quality and quantity of light, water, and air. Here are common problems that are a result of improper environmental conditions.

Poor Lighting Conditions

Some garden plants require up to eight hours of sunlight a day, while others need only a couple of hours for growth. Providing too much or too little sunlight for plants can result in a list of complications that include:

- Delayed or unproductive flowering and fruit (not enough or the wrong type of light)
- Weak, spindly looking plants (not enough light)
- Slow or weak growth (not enough light)
- Leaves that look dried or scorched (too much direct light)

- Discolored leaves (not enough light)

The solutions to these problems are simple and involve adjusting the amount of direct sunlight that the plant receives. A common misconception is that since most houseplants grow successfully in an indoor environment without much thought that garden plants will as well. While it is true that you can successfully grow many garden plants inside, sometimes you need to make adjustments for their extra need for sunlight. This can be done by changing their location to a southern-facing window with ample sun exposure or purchasing grow lights and using them to supplement natural sunlight.

Hydration Problems

Just like with sunlight, plants can be very particular about how much water they need to thrive. Some plants like moist soil, while others prefer their soil to be more on the dry side. Over or under watering garden plants produces a unique set of symptoms that can include;

- Yellowing leaves (too much water)
- Brown or darkened leaf tips (not enough water)
- Inadequate growth (too much or too little water, sometimes due to root rot)

- General wilted appearance (too much or too little water)

If you find you are having any of these issues with your plants, feel the soil and examine the drainage quality of the container that your plant is in. Each plant should have adequate drainage. This means drainage holes at the bottom of the box and a layer of pebbles or other drainage material in the container's bottom below the soil. If you are having trouble keeping your plants adequately watered, consider purchasing an inexpensive automatic watering system. Also, it is worth taking a look at the air quality and humidity levels in your gardening space. Air that is too humid will contribute to overly wet soil. At the same time, not enough humidity might suck the moisture out of your plants prematurely.

Temperature

For best results, indoor garden plants need to be kept at a temperature that is comparable to the climate that they would be exposed to if they were outside. In most cases, plants will thrive between the range of 75°F to 85°F, with a median temperature of about 80°F being the most favorable. Signs that your plants are suffering from being exposed to improper temperatures include:

- Brown leaf tips
- Yellowing leaves
- Defoliation

You can help regulate the temperature of your plants by placing them on a garden heating mat that can be set to maintain a specific temperature. It is best not to substitute household items such as heating pads and electric blankets because of the potential fire hazard of keeping them on for extended periods.

Too Much Fertilizer

Some fertilizer is a good thing; too much fertilizer is a bad thing. An abundance of nitrogen fertilizer can damage plants, rather than encourage their growth. Signs that you could be using too much fertilizer are:

Browning leaves

Plants that overgrow without producing flowers or fruits

The best way to know how much fertilizer to use for your plants is to ask a professional about each plant species, making sure to mention that you are an indoor gardener. Rather than use chemical fertilizers, try sticking to organic or composted fertilizers, including ones made from ordinary household scraps such as organic vegetable material and coffee grounds.

Indoor Gardening Infections and Bacteria

One of the benefits of indoor gardening over outdoor gardening is that, in general, plants grown indoors are relatively healthy and free from disease and pests. This doesn't mean that they are never encountered, however. Plants that are stressed due to poor growing conditions or lack of attentive care are especially susceptible to infections and bacteria. Following are a few of the most common indoor garden infections that you might encounter.

Root and Stem Rot

When plants are overwatered or are not allowed adequate drainage, the opportunity arises for a disease known as root or stem rot. The symptoms of this disease include;

- Soft stems
- Wilted plants
- Decay

- Soft roots, sometimes foul-smelling
- Dark ring on the stem near the soil

The best treatment for root or stem rot is prevention by not overwatering and providing good drainage for your plants. When you see signs of root or stem rot, remove the infected roots, and transfer the plant to clean fresh soil in a new pot.

Mold and Mildew

Occasionally, you may notice that some of your leaves have powdery appearing mildew substances on them. This is a disease that typically can be caught and remedied before it does too much damage to the plant. Signs of a mold or mildew infection include:

- Powdery white or greenish substance appearing on one or multiple leaves

Drooping leaves

To remedy this condition, it is vital to remove all of the infected parts of the plant and transplant them into fresh soil if the existing ground seems to retain too much moisture. Also, you might want to increase the air circulation around the plant by opening windows or turning on a fan to promote the movement of air. Also, make sure that the soil moisture level remains at a level that is not overly saturated.

Leaf Spots

These tiny spots on leaves caused by different fungus and bacteria can damage the leaves to the point that parts of the plant begin to deteriorate. If your plants are suffering from such a condition, you will notice:

- Brown or yellow spots on leaves
- Spots surrounded by what appears to be a halo
- Spots on the leaves that appear to be saturated with wetness

To solve the issue of spots on your leaves, remove the infected leaves and prevent further infection by avoiding spraying or misting anything on the leaves and improving air circulation in the area around the plants.

Chapter 6: Useful Tips

When it comes to gardening, there are a great many errors that growers are prone to making, when they start out. In fact, truth to tell, many gardeners continue to make mistakes despite having acquired years of experience. The most common reason that mistakes are made is due to ignorance. Some people simply think that if they can raise carrots, then they can raise lettuce; or if they can grow an orange tree, then they understand how to take care of mint. This attitude ignores the subtle (and not so subtle) differences between plants, and simply reduces a vast topic into too-rigid a formula. When this happens, dead plants and poor harvests are prone to follow.

1. Every plant is different, and this means that every plant has different needs, though some elements of those needs may be similar to others. Even within a particular kind of plant, the various subspecies may have vastly different environmental needs compared to each other.

2. Researching should be the first step you take before starting with any new plants. There are a great many questions that you should ask when you are first considering planting a type of plant that you have not worked with before. These can often be answered by researching these questions on Google, or through approaching a knowledgeable employee at your local gardening center.

3. Beginners often aim big and plant all sorts of different plants, with the intention of enjoying them on their dinner plate in the near future. What they overlook is the difficulty associated with maintaining multiple types of plants

simultaneously, and how much time and energy it takes to look after a full garden.

4. It is always smarter to start with 1-3 plants and to bring them from seed to harvest, before branching out and increasing the size of your garden. A modest beginning will give you a sense of how much effort it takes to properly grow your fruits, vegetables, or herbs.

5. When you have your plants too close together, their roots begin to fight each other for nutrients. This wastes energy that would be better employed in growing healthy adult plants. Planting too close together will leave you with small, sickly plants. Planting too close together also makes it easier for pests and diseases to spread from one plant to another. They will not need to travel as far, and there are more parts of the plants that are obscured from the scrutiny of the gardener.

6. Signs like discoloration, bumps, or holes in your leaves are telltale signs of either infestation or infection. Many pests can be tricky to spot if you

are not specifically looking for them and, if left untreated, they can kill your plants.

7. Check the soil and the bottom of your leaves to see if any pests are hiding where you cannot see them. Make it a habit to check daily. Infection can spread quickly through a plant, and any infected leaves or branches should be cut off and disposed of outdoors. Dead plant matter around the growing space can introduce harmful bacteria into the environment. You should always clean up and tidy your growing area every day, washing your hands afterward, before you touch your plants again.

Pest and Disease Management

Pests are not things to joke with, as they are always very harmful to living things of different species, from humans to animals and plants. There are very many types of pests. While we may be very used to a few of them, others are not very common. They come in different shapes and sizes, from termites to rodents, insects, fungus, fleas, to feral dogs. They are simply those living things that threaten humans and their environments, stock, or food.

Luckily, it is not difficult to control pests as there are many ways to go about pest control. If you cannot get rid of them, you can reduce their presence in your farm or living environment. Generally, healthy hygiene is the first step to take when trying to control pests. Having your garden close to a dumpster is the first recipe for pests. Even after the dumpster has been moved, you may want to do critical sanitization before starting your garden. It is no news that refuses sites are quick to accumulate insects, rodents, and other pests. You also do not want to have a pool, stagnant water in your garden. Objects like old tires, abandoned water cans, and so on lying around in your garden are also not a good idea.

There is no doubt that you must control pests in your physical environment, your garden, or your workplace. You don't want your family to contract diseases from pests or from pest-infested foods from your garden, just the same way you may not want your plants to be killed by pests. There is no room for compromise here; the health of humans and their foods is critical, to you have to get your pest control measures right.

Methods of Pest Control

Proper Knowledge: You will get frustrated if you think you will have it comfortable fighting with something you know little or nothing about. This is why you must learn about the pests in your garden, their characteristics, and their effects on your plants. When you grasp the nature of the problems you are dealing with, you can create strategies around defeating them. This is one crucial area where you cannot afford to make mistakes as you don't want to develop wrong strategies that may have ripple effects on your plants' health later. Find those areas in your garden infiltrated by these pests and the damages they can cause or have already caused. The good news is that there are now companies dedicated to helping farmers identify problems, their habitat, and their effects. If you think you cannot easily find pests on your own, you can use such companies' services as they will help you curb the potential damages of such problems and help you avoid their further growth or spread.

Chemical Control: This is the pest control method whereby chemical pesticides are used to get rid of diseases, weeds, or pests. This is simply a way of using toxic or poisonous materials/substances on target pests. When these chemical substances are used, plant protection products are also necessary to shield the plants from their harmful effects. This is very important so that the plants don't end up dying with the pests that you are trying to get rid of.

These days, there are many chemical pesticides used in gardens and even dwelling places to get rid of pests. You must always bear in mind that pesticides are dangerous as they can poison the land, food, water, and air. As a matter of fact, pesticides are as harmful to the persons or people applying them as they are to the pests they are to control. The same goes for every other living thing that is close to the area where the pesticide is applied.

There are five different groups of pesticides. They are grouped according to the work they do. There are fungicides, chemicals used to combat fungi, while herbicides are used to get rid of weeds. This pesticide is either applied to the leaves or the weed roots to kill them. Another category of pesticides is insecticides, which, according to the name, are used to kill dangerous insects. There are acaricides, chemicals that are used to guard plants against mites. The last type of pesticides is known as nematicides, used in controlling nematodes that are harmful to plants. Nematicides are used to combat dangerous animals. They are injected through the mouth, inhaled via breathing, or via what is known as a dermal entry, an entrance through the skin.

Before you use any of these pesticides, make sure you go through the instruction on the pack or container to avoid food poisoning or contact with utensils or other items that may lead to poisoning. It isn't abnormal to find it hard to apply pesticides by yourself. If you find yourself in such a condition, don't hesitate to call pest control experts to help you do the work.

Mechanical Control: There's another pest control method, which involves machines and devices to get rid of pests from the garden. This method is known as automatic control. The most common way of carrying out this method is to create a demarcation between the plant and the insect or pest. This is like the physical method of getting rid of and attacking problems to stop their spread and stop them from causing more damage to the plant. The first step to take in this method is removing all items or factors that may cause the spread of pests. Things like garbage where problems gather to find food or shelter until the coast is clear enough for them to attack the garden should be kept far from the park. You may also want to find solutions to potholes, stagnant water, or other water bodies where pests are likely to gather.

Poisoned Bait: Recall that pests are not just insects. There are rodents and other types of problems, but pest control is used to control insects. This is simply a method where rodents are fed poisoned foods. While this method may be very useful in getting rid of rodents, it may also be hazardous because there's the risk of other more giant animals feeding on the poisoned rodents. When they do, they also get poisoned. There've been cases of people who die because they came in contact with poisoned meat or consumed the meat of poisoned animals. If you must adopt this method, you have to be extremely careful as slight mistakes can turn fatal.

Field Burning: This is one of the oldest forms of pest control. It is usually done after harvest, and it involves the burning of the entire field to destroy all the harmful animals and other species as well as the eggs they may have left behind. This method of pest control sanitizes the area to the core.

Trap Cropping: This is one of the most technical methods there are and involves planting trap crops, plants that attract pests so that they are kept away from other plants. With this method, problems gather around the trap crops, so it is easier to control them in one spot using different methods of pest control like pesticides.

Natural Methods of Pest Control

As years go by, gardeners and farmers become more and more concerned about popular, traditional pest control methods as most of them indicate interest in more natural, eco-friendly methods of pest control. While more people are becoming interested in these pest control methods, the question on most people's minds is whether natural ways of pest control work. The truth remains that when done correctly, natural methods of pest control maybe even more effective than popular pesticides. Most professional pest control organizations realize this fact. They opt for procedures like extremely cold or hot temperatures to get rid of insects like bedbugs. There are many types of natural pest control, as there are many ways of adopting these pest control techniques. Here are a few of them:

Organic Method

If you want healthy pest control methods to combat pests without destroying your plants and animals effectively, choose natural organic forms. This is simply a way of using adequate and sufficient predator baits to eliminate pests. The most organic method of pest control is using sodium fluoroacetate. This biodegradable poison is usually mixed with tricks or traps to eliminate very many types of pests. This is also the cheapest method of pest control for highly infected areas. Other forms of organic pest control are highlighted below:

Floating row covers: Floating row covers are used to control different types of pests like aphids, cabbage worms, tomato hornworms, potato beetles, cabbage moths, squash bugs, and many other moving pests. These covers further protect the plants against predators like squirrels, birds, deer, rabbits, etc. They simply shield the plants without causing any harm to them as they also serve as ways of protecting the plants from strong winds and harsh sun. These floating row covers are the most effective ways of protecting vegetables from many types of pests during those times when problems are most potent and can damage the plants. If you have planted crops that don't undergo insect pollination phases, you may leave the row covers for as long as the plant remains in the garden.

Floating row covers reach very far in protecting your plants. You may choose to spread your material over the plants or support the materials with wires or hoops. They can be wrapped around the cages of plants like the tomato plant to shield them. You only have to remember that you need to keep the sides covered so that the pests cannot reach your plants. Once you have dropped the material over the plants, get rocks or boards to hold the edges tightly. If you want to do this more effectively, use the row covers immediately after planting the crops and leaving them there for as long as you believe necessary.

Insecticidal Soaps: You can use insecticidal soaps to save the lives of your crops when soft-bodied pests suddenly infest your garden. These soaps work best on soft-bodied pests like spider mites, aphids, and whiteflies. The soaps take effect by using fatty acid to destroy the cuticles that serve as a shield to insects. Once these cuticles are broken down, the insect gets dehydrated, and they die. For this process to be effective, the soap has to have physical contact with the insect. As the plant continues to produce new leaves or fruits, you have to repeat this process. This is usually between the space of 5 to 7 days.

Before you apply insecticidal soaps to the leaves, make sure that the plant leaves are all wet on both sides. Note that many harsh soaps may cause the plant's leaves to burn, so you have to carefully test every plant to know the types of insecticidal soaps they can accommodate before pouring the soap on all your crops. The soaps are usually sold in their concentrated forms, so they have to be diluted before they are applied. The diluted form of the insecticidal soaps can only last for a few days, so be careful to mix the quantity that is enough for a single application at a time.

Oil Sprays: Oil sprays are also useful in getting rid of pests. One of the most common types of oil sprays used for this purpose is neem oil, which controls different types of beetles and squash bugs. This oil has many natural steroids, so when they are sprayed on the pests, they become less interested in laying eggs. They lose appetite, so their growth is stunted.

Conclusion

Wow! There aren't many words to say besides congratulations at this point! I am sure that your head is swimming with dozens of little facts concerning plants and when to plant them and how to plant them.

If you already have a plan, I hope this guide gave you some great tips on expansion, and the best vegetables to grow. Granted, you learn a lot through doing, but having adequate information can make it easier for you to avoid simple mistakes from the beginning or be aware of what to look out for.

At this point, you should have a basic understanding of vegetable gardening, what goes into building one, how it works to maintain your plants, and the best type of plants to start off planting in your garden. That's a lot of information! Has anyone told you they're proud of you for getting this far in your vegetable gardening journey? Because I am proud of you!

I encourage you to keep this guide and circle back to it when you need references for some items. For example, if you ever decide to expand you currently have, this guide offers some great things to keep in mind before moving forward with an expansion. You can grow with your plants in knowledge, but there will always be something good about coming back to the basics.

I hope that you can now tell your tomatoes apart from your strawberries and that all the finer parts of the greenhouse make sense to you. It doesn't matter if you're using a greenhouse box or an entire greenhouse that feeds a family or a city, you will continue to learn as you plant every day.

This book focused on imparting the correct vegetable gardening knowledge to you and allowing you to be empowered to construct your own garden. Garden kits can easily be bought from gardening companies or hardware stores and built yourself as well! Practice your building skills and if you run into trouble call the experts for some advice. The best way to know all the ins and outs of your garden is to be present for every decision from what hardware you use to build the vegetable garden, to how exactly it is put together. Remember to leave yourself the option to expand if you need to.

You got an overall sense of what you could begin to plant in your garden. Ultimately, this is a personal decision, fueled by how much time you have to dedicate to your garden, the climate you keep in your greenhouse, and the types of fruits and vegetables that your family likes to eat.

Hopefully, this guide carries you into some productive planting and growing! There's a lot to learn when it comes to gardening. Good luck and happy growing!

COMPANION PLANTING FOR VEGETABLES

THE BEST TECHNIQUES AND SECRETS FOR AN ABUNDANCE OF VEGETABLES IN THE HOME GARDEN

Bradley Gray

Introduction

Companion planting not only works, but it has also proven itself to be smart gardening. If you study and research it, you will discover you can group certain plants that encourage each other's growth and help to attract the good insects and keep the bad ones out. It might be the aroma or odor of a plant that protects its neighbors from pests, or the plant's roots might secrete pest-deterring substances. On occasion, it might be both. Either way, companion planting is a very good thing.

History has shown us that the early European settlers planted corn and beans together, as they were shown to do so by Native Americans. The cornstalk provides a structure that the bean vines can then climb. This clever arrangement allows two crops to grow in the same space. Not only do the corn and beans grow well together, but the beans will also attract beneficial insects. These insects will eat any pests that are drawn to the corn. Because beans are members of the legume family, they also release nitrogen in the soil, allowing any plants nearby to utilize it.

Another example of a symbiotic relationship is the combination of tomatoes and marigolds. This is thought to repel nematodes, which are harmful to plants. As the repellent builds in the soil over time, you have to plant the "smelly" marigold flowers with the tomatoes for a minimum of 1 to 2 years to get the full benefit. Other options for companion planting with tomatoes include carrots and parsley.

Choosing Companion Plants

Basil is thought to increase the flavor of tomatoes while it repels both disease and insects. Basil also benefits from planting with asparagus, oregano, and peppers, but don't plant it near sage.

Beet plants do well growing with onions, lettuce, brassicas, and bush beans. Plant garlic with beets to enhance the growth and flavor of the beet vegetable.

Borage is loaded with minerals and its flowers invite parasitic wasps and beneficial pollinators. It is thought to boost the pest and disease resistance of any plant growing besides the borage.

Brassicas grow best when planted with potatoes, marigolds, nasturtiums, bush beans, beets, dill, and onions, but do not grow them near eggplant, peppers, tomatoes, or strawberries.

Carrots are happy around peas, onions, and lettuce. Do not plant them near tomatoes, which stunt the carrots' growth and they also do not like being grown by dill, brassicas, or potatoes.

Cucumbers are good neighbors to sunflowers, nasturtiums, marigolds, onions, corn, lettuce, peas, and beans, but do not grow them with or near potatoes. If you plant radishes in each cucumber hill, they are thought to be repellent against, or at least confuse, cucumber beetles; they also repel flea beetles. The radish plants must flower to attract beneficial insects.

Fennel should be planted only with dill, which is strong enough to stand up to it. Fennel plants exude a substance that inhibits the growth of all other nearby plants.

Lettuce does well near radishes, strawberries, onions, cucumbers, carrots, beets, and beans. But lettuce does not do well when grown near parsley or brassicas. Planting mint repels slugs from eating your lettuce.

Lovage is thought to improve the flavor and growth of whatever you plant near it.

Onions, along with other alliums like shallots, leeks, garlic, and chives protect a large number of plants including roses but do not plant them near asparagus, peas, or beans.

Both kinds of parsley grow well with carrots, roses, asparagus, and tomatoes.

Peas and beans enhance growth in many plants including strawberries, radishes, lettuce, eggplant, cucumbers, corn, carrots, and brassicas. Allegedly summer savory repels bean beetles and improves flavor and growth in beans. Do not Grow onions with peas or beans because they stunt each other's growth.

Peppers, both hot and sweet, are good companions to onions and basil.

Tomato growth can be improved when you grow them with nasturtiums, marigolds, parsley, basil, and onions. Do not plant tomatoes with brassicas because both plants will suffer. Do not plant tomatoes with potatoes because both are susceptible to late blight.

To have enough effect, companion plants have to be grown in adequate quantities. One lonely summer savory plant at the end of each row of beans will not be as effective as interspersing them along each side and throughout each row.

Learning what to plant in a vegetable garden, and how to take care of them so they produce a bountiful harvest, is not all that hard.

With proper planning, you can enjoy the fruits of your labor from a beautiful garden. You can also do that without having to spend hours and hours tending it. If you plant a garden that has both vegetables and flowers, you have already combined natural companions. This can turn a piece of unattractive piece of soil into an attractive piece of landscape.

Chapter 1: Why Companion Planting?

Companion planting is the practice of planting different garden species close together, rather than keeping each type of plant in its specific row or corner of the garden. Different kinds of plants interact with each other and with the natural environment in beneficial ways.

Why Use Companion Gardening?

Thousands of years ago, our ancestors discovered that if they specialized in growing just a few crops, they could increase the amount of food they produced. But planting the same crop year after year in the same field led to problems. Every plant species needs slightly different nutrients, and these get depleted quickly if the same crops are planted successively. Diseases that target specific crops can also be left behind in the soil from season to season. Crop rotation was invented to minimize these negative effects. Farmers across the globe have also known for thousands of years that planting different species in the same area could improve the health and the yields of their crops.

During the Green Revolution in the mid-20th century, farmers all over the world were encouraged to plant newly developed disease-resistant crops in large monoculture operations. Essentially the same crop would be planted year after year in the same field, with the help of chemical fertilizers, pesticides, and agricultural machinery. There's no doubt that this practice fed millions or even billions of people who would have otherwise gone hungry. However, progress has come at a cost. Traditional agricultural practices often create habitat for wild animals and plants, but these are lost with industrial farming. Lack of biodiversity also means a lack of nutritional variety, and many people are suffering from malnutrition even though they may consume more calories than before. Pesticides have harmed wild plants and animals, as well as causing health problems such as cancer in humans.

More and more people are turning to traditional gardening and farming techniques as a way to combat these problems. The future of global industrial farming may be too big a problem for you to contend with, but even if you only have a balcony or an urban patio to work with, you can experience the satisfaction of growing a little bit of your food.

Here are some of the benefits that companion planting can bring to your garden.

Structural Support

Taller, sun-loving plants can provide shade for shorter plants. In West Africa, cocoa farmers plant new trees in the shade of plantain and cassava plants, both of which are also food crops. Planting coffee in the shade of natural forests in Central America and Africa benefits both the coffee crop and the ecosystem.

Companion plants can also act as a living trellis for a climbing plant. Pole beans can climb up corn stalks, and sunflowers or Jerusalem artichokes can act as support for climbing beans, small cucumbers, and other vine plants. The traditional Native North American combination of corn, beans, and squash, known as the Three Sisters, uses corn as a trellis for beans.

The Three Sisters example also shows another structural use of companion plants and living mulch. The low-growing squash in this grouping helps guard against drying of the soil and helps keep weeds away, just as regular mulch would. Vetch and clover are also frequently used as living mulches.

Nitrogen Fixing

All green plants require nitrogen to grow and survive. Most plants need to use nitrogen that is already in the soil, but a few can take it straight from the atmosphere, and even "fix" it in the soil where other plants can use it. Beans (and all legumes) are nitrogen fixers, which brings us back to the Three Sisters example yet again. Clover, vetch, and alfalfa are other good examples of nitrogen-fixing plants. These plants provide a small number of nitrates to the soil while they are living, but it's after they die and decompose that you get the biggest benefit. This is why nitrogen fixers are often planted at the end of the growing season and plowed into the soil before the new planting. These crops are sometimes called "green manure."

Attracting or Repelling Insects

Some plants seem to keep pests away. Marigolds and alliums (onions and garlic) are often used for this purpose. Other plants are good at attracting beneficial insects to your garden. Asters, cosmos, and many other flowers provide a home for insect predators that feed on aphids and other pests. They also bring in pollinators such as bees and butterflies. Trap cropping is another way to use companion plants to control the insects in your garden: you include some plants especially for the insects to eat so that they leave your important plants alone. Nasturtiums are often used to keep aphids and whiteflies away from your garden plants. Planting nightshade can successfully lure certain potato bugs away from your potato plants.

Allelopathy

Allelopathy refers to the ability some plants have to produce chemicals that inhibit the growth of other plants. This is important to companion gardening in two ways. First of all, you can avoid combining crops that interfere with each other. Secondly, you can include plants that inhibit the growth of weeds, reducing the amount of time you have to spend removing weeds. Asters can inhibit ragweed, and ryegrass can help keep several aggressive weeds under control.

Increasing Yield

Some plants seem to produce more when they are planted together for reasons that nobody fully understands. Tomatoes and basil don't just taste good together: if you plant them together you may get a better yield from both plants.

There are also less mysterious ways that companion planting can help you increase your yield. If you have a small space, you can plant fast-growing plants like radishes next to slower-growing eggplants or peppers. Plants with shallow roots (such as lettuce) can share space with deep-rooted plants like carrots. This way you can get two crops in the space that you would normally devote to one crop.

Aesthetics

The wild beauty of a companion garden can be an end in itself for many people. Imagine a vegetable garden with a variety of foliage colors and textures side-by-side, and with colorful flowers interspersed, visited by bumblebees and butterflies. Compare this image with monotonous rows of vegetables separated by bare earth (or more likely, weeds) and you'll see why so many people are attracted to companion planting.

Companion Planting Strategies

Companion planting can be used in several ways in the garden. Every time you turn around, it seems someone is coming up with a new way to use companion plants to their benefit.

Here are just some of the many companion planting strategies that can be employed to help gardeners get the most from their crops:

- Complimentary planting. The act of planting two plants close to one another that will bestow benefits upon each other.

- Cover crops. These are crops planted to act as ground cover or living mulch. Planting cover crops at the end of the gardening season will prevent soil erosion, decrease the impact of water runoff during the rainy season and add organic material to the soil when the cover crop is turned under. Choosing the right type of cover crop is key to ensuring a plot of land continues producing well into the future.

- Nutrition planting. Some plants fix certain nutrients into the soil as they grow. Others release nutrients into the soil after they die. Nutrition planting places plants nearby that are ready to take full advantage of the nutrients being released into the soil.

- Succession planting. This is a spin on nutrition planting in which plants that benefit one another are planted one after another. For example, bush beans fix nitrogen into the soil. Corn needs nitrogen to grow. Grow bush beans early in the season and turn them into the soil after harvest. Plant corn in the same area to take full advantage of the nitrogen released into the soil.

- Pattern disruption. Plant row after row of similar crops and a single plant infested with pests or disease can spell doom for the rest of your crop as the next plant is only a short hop away. Break plants up by adding other plants between them that are not susceptible to the same pests and diseases and you have just made it a lot harder for them to spread.

- Square-foot gardening. Divide a small garden into 4' X 4' planting areas and divide those areas into plots of 1 square foot apiece and you have got a square-foot garden. Companion plants are important in square-foot gardens because you are trying to grow a lot of plants in a limited amount of space.

A plant that benefits a nearby plant is good. A plant that benefits multiple nearby plants while benefiting from them is even better. The best companions bestow multiple benefits upon one another and are mutually beneficial. Finding a group of plants that all benefit each other in multiple ways is one of the best ways to ensure you have a bumper crop.

Full Sun vs. Partial Shade

One of the biggest decisions you are going to have to make is whether you are going to grow a full sun or a partial shade garden. If you are limited in space, this decision may have already been made for you and you are going to have to work with what you have got. The amount of sun and shade an area gets is one of the major determining factors of the types of plants that can be grown there.

Most fruits and vegetables prefer full sun, so if you are looking to grow a produce garden, that is the way to go.

That is not to say they all prefer sitting in the middle of a desert baking in hot sunlight. Full sun is defined as at least 6 hours of sunlight per day, while some plants need as many as 8 to 10 hours per day to thrive. Trying to grow plants that require full sun in an area that gets less exposure to the sun than this will be an exercise in frustration. The plants may grow, but yields will be reduced, and they will be more susceptible to attack from pests and disease.

Partial shade or partial sun implies a plant needs less sunlight and can get by on 3 to 6 hours of sunlight per day. These plants do best when they are shaded from the sun in the afternoon when It is at its peak. Placing a plant that prefers partial shade or partial sun in an area that gets full sunlight can scorch the plant when temperatures start to climb, causing it to wilt or even die.

Full shade means relatively little sunlight. There may be a small handful of plants you can grow in full shade, but without much light, you are going to be very limited. If you want to plant fruit and vegetables, you are going to have to find another spot.

Most vegetables, fruits, and herbs prefer full sunlight. If you have a garden that only gets partial sunlight, you are going to have to select plants that can be grown with only partial sunlight. There is not a whole lot you can do to increase the amount of sunlight an area gets short of chopping down trees, moving mountains, or tearing down buildings. Reflective mulches can be used to reflect sunlight up to plants, but the effect is minimal.

Lettuce, spinach, radishes, and some varieties of strawberries are well-suited to partially shaded garden areas. Other crops like peas and potatoes will grow in partial shade, but yields will be reduced. To be clear, these plants will still need sunlight to grow—they just do not need as much as some of the needier plants.

Those looking to grow plants that require partial shade in a full sun location have a handful of options at their disposal. For one, you can build a structure that provides shade during certain times of the day. It is best to build a shade that provides relief from the afternoon sun, as opposed to one that provides shade in the morning. Afternoon sunlight is hotter and more likely to damage plants than morning sunlight. Another option is to set up latticework through which the sun can shine. Your plants will get sunlight throughout the day but will not be exposed to the constant heat of the sun. Some plants will do better than others with this technique, so experiment to find out what works best.

You may be wondering what all this has to do with companion planting. Some plants grow tall or have large leaves that spread out that can be used to provide shade to smaller plants. The larger plants can be planted as companion plants to smaller plants that need partial shade. Corn, sunflowers, tomatoes, and artichokes can all be planted to provide shade for smaller plants. Trellises plants like pole beans and grapes are also a good way to provide dappled sunlight, which is the light that is filtered through the leaves of the trellised plant.

These larger sun-loving plants can be planted to provide shade for plants like cabbage, broccoli, and cauliflower that do not do well when temperatures start to climb as summer approaches. Smaller plants like carrots, cucumbers, and lettuce can also benefit from being planted in the shade of a taller plant if the taller plants do not surround them and completely block out the sun.

Trees can be used to provide shade, but you must be careful not to use a variety of trees that are going to grow to great heights and completely block sunlight from reaching your garden. If trees are already present and are providing too much shade, you may be able to top them or prune them back to ensure your garden gets ample sunlight.

Chapter 2: The Benefits of Companion Planting

Companion planting is one of the best ways to increase crop harvest and minimize pest infestation just naturally. The benefits of companion planting are many. Below is a list of the major roles that the style adds to the garden and the crops in general.

Hedged Crop Yield

This is the plain simple truth that when using companion cropping when one crop fails the other will cover up for the loss quite fast. This is for instance when there is a cabbage moth butterfly attack in a field. While sweet corn may not be able to stop the crop from dying or drying up, it will shield the farmer from a permanent loss.

The whole idea is to have a system that will assure the farmer of some degree of produce irrespective of the prevailing pests, disease, and weather conditions. This gives more assurance for the farmer that there will be some output from the farm than when he just has to grow a single crop. This shielding of the farmer from epidemics will bring about an overall reduction of risk in the income of the farm and help the farmer benefit more from his farm as a business.

Helper Interaction For The Crops

When grown together, crops can help each other grow to a healthier garden as opposed to when planted in a pure lot alone. This is especially so when the farmer needs to grow crops that cannot thrive physically, physiologically, or chemically on their own. For instance, beans are known to start rotting early and lower yields when not propped. When grown with maize though, this forms a natural stake that increases the yield of the beans.

Since some plants like legumes are good at fixing nitrogen to the soil, they can be of use to others that do not have that ability. Now nitrogen is a volatile mineral and whenever it is exposed to sunlight it goes into the air in the form of gasses such as nitrogen oxides. The processes of legumes in the above example eventually help the maize plants have access to better and more nutritious soil.

Finally, since there is very wide variation as to the crops that feed on certain minerals and those that do not, there is eventually no compctition of nutrients in most scenarios and the crops end up running after different minerals in the soil. This will drive the farmer's prospects of higher-income further while keeping the input requirements constant on the farm. A great example is a scenario where both maize and beans need different minerals and so their growth in the same garden does not affect each other negatively. However, at the end of the day, the farmer who had nothing to lose by planting both sides by side will have higher produce and more income.

Protection Of Weaker Plants

Another key advantage of companion cropping is really to protect the crops from elements of nature and also organisms. For instance, if blown too much by the wind, beans often lose their flowers and do not yield any produce for the shed flowers. When grown with maize side by side, the beans will be shielded from strong winds thus allowing them to pollinate normally and yield a higher harvest.

Apart from natural calamities, companion cropping also helps crops that are predisposed to attack by predators to be protected. In tropical environments, for instance, elephants are fond of feeding on pumpkins and they can smell them from as far as 50 kilometers. Monkeys on the other hand love to eat tomatoes. Planting tomatoes and pumpkins intercropped with chili as a companion crop will however deal with the elephant and monkey menace permanently. Monkeys and elephants detest the smell of pepper.

Finally, protection also comes from the companion plants from certain smaller pests. Cabbage butterfly worms are very likely to attack broccoli and cabbages, but planting French marigolds on the farm will keep off the pests. Other methods of controlling pests include planting companion crops that distract the pests, planting companion crops that repel the pests, or even planting crops that kill the pests. Nematodes for instance die within hours of eating garlic, and thus garlic is a great protective plant for many varieties of farm crops.

Suppression Of Pests Without Chemicals

As indicated above, some plants put off some pests that feed on one plant and thus are an effective way of protecting the companion plant. This is a simple form of organic farming that reduces the necessity of chemical use in the farm leading to more healthy produce that is free of pesticides and herbicides. Companion cropping also reduces the effect of many weeds on the

Trap Cropping

Distracting pests from certain crops and drawing them to others can also help some crops that have a lower attraction of pests than others. This is a method that has been used in the past to deal with pests organically. A great example is wheat versus fodder grasses. Fodder grasses are grown along with the wheat so that they distract the pests from feeding on the wheat stalks and feed instead on the grass stalks. At the end of the day, the wheat remains healthy and fit at the expense of grass that will later be used as feed for animals.

Pattern Disruption

Unlike monoculture, it has controlled pest spread. Pattern disruption is a method of disease control that maximizes moving pests from crop to crop hard. Put simply, consider a grasshopper flying randomly from crop to crop in a field seeking a plant A. If the field has a monoculture of plant A alone, then it will be a poor idea to have it that way. The whole crop will be devoured by the pests in a quick succession of events.

However, picture scenario B. When crop A has been inter-planted with crops B, C, and D, it becomes hard for the grasshopper to spot the correct plant. If it hits two or so misses in a row without finding the correct plant A, it may eventually give up and go to another location. This is known as pattern disruption. The good thing is that it is not only effective on pests, but also diseases. Some diseases that attack fields as an epidemic are rather stoppable when strategies such as companion cropping are employed.

Organic Gardening

A great way to have organic gardening is always by companion cropping. Many gardeners who wish to eliminate chemical pests and disease control in their gardens will opt for companion cropping as the right method of action. That said, it is also good to note that organic gardening though a branch of agriculture on its own and with its features, rides heavily on the advantage of companion cropping to achieve natural control of pests and diseases.

Reduce The Crowding Of Crops

This is a common practice among many gardeners. While crops are not fewer per square meter or foot, companion gardening reduces the number of crops of one type in a small space. When this is done, there is an increased distance between one crop and the other of the same type. Eventually, there is an apparent reduction in congestion in the garden.

Low maintenance of the garden

Even when not practicing organic gardening, the effects of companion gardening will be felt by the garden in a big way. The first thing here at play is that there will be fewer pests to deal with so the chemicals and pesticides budget will be kind of low. Since the ground cover is optimum, there will be no need for the application of artificial mulch and other related expenses. Again since there are crops that assist each other to grow and add nutrients to the ground, there will be a lesser need to add fertilizers. This is a huge determinant of the budget implications arising from the growth of a healthy farm.

Nutrient Management

Nutrient management is an aspect of the farm that many gardeners have to keep worrying about in the course of the seasons. When growing only one variety of crops, it is always a great thing to test the soils regularly to see if the balance of nutrients is good. Remember that many crops take in only one variety of nutrients thus the rest of them are underutilized. This may lead to the soils becoming either acidic or saline depending on the crop that has been grown most in the past seasons. However, with companion cropping, it becomes very easy to manage the nutrients on the farm. Since different crops are feeding on different minerals, it is very easy to regulate the mineral and nutrient content in the garden.

Chapter 3: Companion Vegetables

This offers you an in-depth look at how to plant various vegetables and the best and worst companion plants to go with them. Remember that most vegetables like nutrient-rich soil full of well-rotted compost and mulches. Even if the individual plant instructions do not mention this fact, make sure your garden bed is richly prepared before beginning. There are a few vegetables that do well in sandy beds, like carrots, but most do better in well dug over dirt that has been enriched with nutrients in preparation for the long growing season. All beds will also benefit from additional nutrients throughout the growing season.

The following are guidelines you can follow, but take the time to make this fun. Mix up the planting and interplant carrots with beets and radishes or try planting kohlrabi with both to take advantage of the nutrients at the surface level versus deeper root levels. Vegetable gardening can be a fun and rewarding experience.

Asparagus

Asparagus prefers to grow in the same spot year after year, so pick a full-sun location for best results or partial shade in a spot where it will not need to be disturbed. You will need to purchase asparagus crowns from your local garden center or nursery catalog. The crown will have a strong root system but the top growth will be dormant. Plant the crowns in early spring for most locations; if you live in a warmer climate, you can plant in late winter. The asparagus will need to be planted deep so make a trench approximately 6 to 7 inches deep. Spread the bottom of the trench with wood ashes or bone meal and compost if you have it. There will be instructions on the asparagus when you purchase it, so make sure you read and follow them.

In general, soaking the roots first, preferably in compost tea, is a good start. Then lay them on their side in the trench approximately 1 foot apart. Make sure the rows are 3 to 4 feet apart. You will fill in the trench slowly as the sprouts appear but only cover the stalks and be sure to leave the foliage uncovered. With time, the trench will fill in and the asparagus foliage will now be above ground level. It is important to be diligent with the weeding and you should aim to lay down mulch once the trench is filled in.

Asparagus has many companion plants, including the family of aster flowers, dill, coriander, basil, comfrey, and marigolds, which will deter beetles. Parsley appears to increase the growth of both plants when they are grown together. Tomatoes and asparagus help each other; tomatoes protect against asparagus beetles and a chemical in the asparagus juice deters nematodes from tomato plants. There are no known bad companions for asparagus; however, these plants do better when they are not close to an onion, garlic, or potatoes.

Beans

There are different types of beans available, like snap, dry, and bush. Some will have different companions, both good and bad. Some basics apply to all types of beans. Plant in a full-sun location or partial shade if you live in hot climates. Sow seeds only after the danger of frost has passed. For scarlet runner beans, which are climbers, supply support of some kind. Thin the seedlings to 5 or 6 inches apart, but leave slightly more space for pole beans.

All beans can enrich the soil with nitrogen. They all do well when planted with carrots, cauliflower, peas, radishes, potatoes, strawberries, the brassica family, chard, and corn, and they are of great benefit to cucumbers and cabbage. Summer savory is another good companion to beans as it improves the beans' growth and flavor and deters the bean beetles. Marigolds, rosemary, and nasturtiums also deter bean beetles.

Bad companions for beans include garlic, onion, and shallots as they appear to stunt the plants' growth. They are not happy planted close to gladiolas. Beans are prone to diseases, but crop rotation will prevent most of them. There are also companions specific to individual types of beans.

Bush beans

Bush beans, a shrub variety of the snap bean, do well with celery if planted at the ratio of one celery plant to six bush beans. Bush beans do well close to celery and leeks but only if there are only one or two bean plants there. If more than this is planted, then none of them do well. Bush beans will give and receive benefits when planted with strawberries and cucumbers. Bush beans are a bad companion to fennel and onions.

Pole beans

Pole beans, a climbing variety of beans like the scarlet runner beans, do particularly well with corn, summer savory, and radish.

They do not particularly like beets. They make bad companions with onions, beets, cabbage, eggplant, kohlrabi, and sunflowers.

Broad beans

Broad beans also called fava beans or horse beans, produce large, flat pods with large beans inside. They are excellent companions for corn, potato, cucumbers, strawberry, celery, and summer savory. They are bad companions with onions.

Beets

Beets are an easy-to-grow crop that prefers a full-sun location and well-tilled soil with good drainage. They germinate well and will need to be thinned to 4 inches apart with rows at least 2 feet apart. Beets are great for the garden as they add minerals to the soil.

Beets are good companions for lettuce, onions, kohlrabi, and the brassica family. Mint, garlic (which improves the beet's flavor), and catnip help beets grow. If you do not want to plant mints around the beets, you can use mint foliage as mulch. Beets are bad companions to pole beans and give mixed results next to bush beans.

Broccoli

Broccoli grows best in full sun or partial shade in well-drained soil. In terms of minimizing disease, plant broccoli where no other brassicas (including cabbage, Brussels sprouts, kohlrabi, and cauliflower) have been planted in the last two years as per crop rotation rules. Broccoli is a large plant and can reach 3 feet in height so the seeds or nursery seedlings should be planted 18 inches apart after the danger of frost has passed. If they do not form heads (broccoli florets) properly, they are deficient in lime, phosphorus, or potash. You can purchase these nutrients at your garden center and add them to your broccoli plants.

Broccoli, like all the brassicas, does well with aromatic plants including dill, which improves the plant's growth and health. Broccoli is a good companion to beets, celery, chard, cucumber, lettuce, onion, potato, and spinach. Flea beetles like broccoli so plant Chinese Daikon and Snow Belle radishes to attract flea beetles away from the broccoli.

Do not plant close to tomatoes, strawberries, pole beans, peppers, or mustards as they are bad companions.

Cabbage

Cabbage needs to spend at least half the time in the shade. You can grow from seed or purchase the plant from a nursery to get a jump on the season. Insects like young cabbages so consider covering the plants with a light-weight cloth when they are first growing. They love compost, fertilizer, and water. If the cabbage's florets do not form properly, the plant is deficient in lime, phosphorus, or potash and you should purchase some from your local garden supply store to add to your beds.

Cabbage, like all the brassica family, does well with aromatic plants including dill, white sage, peppermint, and rosemary to help repel cabbage flies. Celery and dill improve cabbage's health and growth. Clover will reduce native cabbage aphids and cabbage worms. Other good companions include onions, potatoes, hyssop, thyme, and southernwood. Wormwood repels white cabbage butterflies. Tansy deters cabbage worm and cutworm, and thyme deters cabbage worm. Nasturtium deters bugs, beetles, and aphids from cabbage.

Bad companions for cabbage are strawberries, tomatoes, peppers, lettuce, eggplants, rue, grapes, and pole beans.

Carrots

Carrots prefer full sun and need a very loose, preferably sandy soil for the roots to grow easily downward. If your soil is high in lime, humus, and potash, you will have sweeter-tasting carrots. Low nitrogen levels in the soil will decrease the flavor of your carrots. Sow seeds directly into the garden several weeks ahead of the last frost (in warm climates you can sow in fall, winter, and spring). Sow seeds around ½ inch deep and thin to 3 to 4 inches apart. Thin early before the roots entwine and are careful to not damage the remaining plants.

Plant onions, leeks, rosemary, and sage to deter the carrot fly. Other good companions include lettuce, onions, chives, beans (which are a good source of nitrogen and can help increase your carrots' flavor), peas, peppers, radish, and tomatoes. Tomatoes can stunt the carrot's growth but they will have a great flavor. Bad companions for the carrot are dill and parsnip. If you want to use carrots to attract insects, they need to be able to flower, so plant a few carrots to leave them in the ground instead of harvesting them for eating.

Cauliflower

Cauliflower likes a full-sun location in well-drained soil. Purchase nursery stock to get a jump on the season or sow outdoors after the danger of frost has passed. Sow in small clusters of several seeds but once they have sprouted, keep only the strongest cauliflower plants. Keep the plants moist when they are young.

For growing instructions and companions, see cabbage as most members of the brassica family have similar growing requirements.

Celery

Celery needs to have a lot of sunshine but can have partial sun for half of the day. Celery requires rich, moist soil. It is easiest to work with plants from the nursery that you can transplant into the garden when there is no danger of frost. Plant 8 to 10 inches apart and be generous with compost and water over the growing season.

Good companion plants for celery include beans, leeks, onions, spinach, tomato, and the brassica family. Garlic and chives help keep aphids away from celery. If bush beans and celery grow together, they will strengthen each other. Friends of celery include cosmos, daisies, and snapdragons. Bad companions for celery are corn, lettuce, and aster flowers.

Chard

Chard is an easy-to-grow vegetable. It prefers full sunlight unless you live in a hot climate where they prefer partial shade. Well-drained soil with compost helps chard produce well. For most climates, sow the seeds in the spring and thin to 8 inches apart when the seedlings are about 6 inches high. You can either eat these seedlings or transport them to another spot in the garden.

Good companions for chard include beans, brassica family members, and onions. There are no known bad companions.

Corn

Corn likes full sun and a rich, well-draining soil covered in the mulch. Sow several seeds in a hill approximately 1 inch deep and 6 inches apart. When seedlings are close to 4 inches tall, thin them to 1 foot apart. Corn needs a steady supply of water and mulch.

Corn helps beans when grown together (as in the Three Sisters example) and sunflowers, legumes, peanuts, squash, cucumbers, melons, amaranth, white geranium, lamb's quarters, morning glory, parsley, and potatoes all help corn. Marigolds help to deter the Japanese beetle away from corn. Planting radishes around corn and letting them go to seed deters an insect called a corn borer, which is known to be a pest for several crops. Bad companions for corn are tomatoes and celery. Pigweed is said to raise nutrients from the deeper earth level to a place where the corn can reach them.

Cucumber

Cucumbers like full sun and can also do well with afternoon shade. Seeds are sown several inches deep a couple of weeks after the danger of frost has passed and once the soil has warmed slightly. Plant the bush varieties approximately 1½ feet apart and the vine varieties 2 to 3 feet apart.

Cucumbers have many good companions including corn, beans, sunflowers, peas, beets, and carrots. Radishes can deter cucumber beetles. Keeping dill close to cucumbers attracts beneficial predators and cucumbers attract ground beetles. Nasturtiums improve the cucumbers' growth and flavor. Bad companions for cucumbers include tomatoes and sage.

Eggplant

Eggplant loves heat, so plant it where it can have full sun. It is easiest to purchase started plants then transplant them when there is no longer any danger of frost. It is preferable to wait a week or two after frost has passed to allow the soil to warm up. There are dwarf and standard varieties of eggplant. Plant the standard versions approximately 1½ to 2 feet apart and the dwarf varieties can be 1 to 1½ feet apart. Tie the taller varieties to stakes to keep the fruit from touching the ground.

Good companions for the eggplant include amaranth, peas, spinach, and marigolds, which deter nematodes. Eggplant helps beans and peppers. They are good to plant with corn as they deter raccoons from eating the corn and the corn protects the eggplant from a virus that causes wilt. Bad companions for eggplants are pole beans, fennel, and potatoes. There are mixed results when planted with aromatic herbs.

Horseradish

This is an easy plant to grow and will take over your garden in no time. Find a corner away from most of the plants and consider planting horseradish in containers. It is easiest to purchase a small plant from the nursery and it will grow in most conditions. Plant 1 foot apart and bury the top of the root 4 inches below the surface. Make sure you water this plant well.

If you grow this plant in a container, you can move the containers around. Keep 1 plant in the potato patch to deter the blister beetle and help deter the Colorado potato beetle. Horseradish also improves the potatoes' resistance to disease. If you are going to plant it in the potato patch, be sure to dig it up and remove it in the fall to prevent the plant from spreading.

Kohlrabi

Kohlrabi is a cooler weather vegetable that can be planted for both spring and fall crops. Plant in full sun and well-drained soil. Sow seeds outside four weeks before the last frost. Plant the seeds ½ inch deep and 3 inches apart but thin them to 6 inches when the seedlings are several inches high, which will not take very long as these plants are very fast growing.

Kohlrabi is a good companion with cucumbers, beets, onions, and chives and appears to help protect members of the mustard family. It is a bad companion to strawberries, tomatoes, peppers, and pole beans.

Leeks

Leeks like a full-sun location that offers well-drained soil. It is easiest to buy leek plants to transplant into the garden around the time of the last frost. Place the seedlings approximately 6 inches apart. Set the plants closer together if you are planting long, thin-stemmed varieties or set them wider apart for thick-stemmed varieties. (Always check the package for specific planting instructions.) Make a hole and set the seedling down so that only an inch of the top of the plant is exposed. Fill it in loosely with soil.

Leeks will improve the growth of celery, onions, and apple trees. Carrots help leeks by repelling carrot flies. Bad companions for leeks are legumes including beans and peas.

Lettuce

Lettuce does best with a mixture of sun and shade. It does not like the extreme heat and will need shade during the hottest months or else it will go to seed. Sow the seeds outdoors once the ground has thoroughly thawed and can be worked. If you purchased plants, set them approximately 1 foot apart (this may vary based on the variety so read the label) and they can be sown several times for a lettuce supply all summer.

Lettuce does well when close to radish, onions, kohlrabi, beans (both bush and pole), cucumbers, carrots, strawberries, beets, and sunflowers. Chives and garlic are great deterrents of aphids so plant them close to lettuce. Mints like hyssop and sage repel slugs so plant these plants close to your lettuce if slugs are a problem in your area. Lettuce is a bad companion to celery, cabbage, and parsley.

Onions

Onions are another plant where it helps to purchase plants at a nursery instead of starting the plant from seeds. You can transplant onions into your garden up to two months before the last frost is expected. Any earlier than this and it could be too cold for them. They like a partial to sunny spot and appreciate compost. Make sure the soil is dug over well to allow for good bulb development and weed constantly in the early growth stage as the weeds can crowd out the young onion plants. As the bulbs grow, make sure to keep them covered if they start to push out of the ground.

Good companions for the onion include all the brassicas, beets, lettuce, tomatoes, summer savory, leeks, kohlrabi, dill, lettuce, and tomatoes. Plant onions in the strawberry patch to help the strawberries stay healthy and fight off disease. Pigweed can raise the nutrients from subsoil and makes them available to the onions. Bad companions for onions are peas, beans, and parsley.

Chapter 4: Perfect Combinations

Some plants work best with each other, which is why they are considered "perfect combinations". Here are some of that you may want to try yourself.

- Cabbage and Tomatoes. Tomatoes can repel the Diamondback Moth larvae which are infamous for chewing cabbage leaves and leaving large holes in them.

- Nasturtiums and Cucumbers. Cucumbers make use of Nasturtiums as trellises while Nasturtiums can repel the dreaded cucumber beetles. They also serve as a natural habitat for ground beetles and spiders which are predatory insects.

- Ragweed/Pigweed and Peppers. Ragweed and Pigweed are good weeds that can make the soil fertile and can protect plants from being infested by pests.

- Corn and Beans. This combination has been used for thousands of years, and they are both able to attract beneficial insects such as leaf beetles and leaf horns. Aside from that, they also provide shade and trellis to each other, making sure that they both grow well and become beneficial for humans.

- Dill and Cabbage. They support each other in the sense that dill attracts wasps that eat pests and worms, making sure that the cabbages grow without holes.

- Chives and Roses. Garlic repels the pests that feed on roses, and they also look great when they are planted next to each other.

- Tall Flowers and Lettuce. Tall flowers such as Cleomes and Nicotiana give lettuce shade.

- Sweet Alyssum and Potatoes. Tiny flowers of sweet alyssum attract predatory wasps and also act as a shade for the potatoes.

- Catnip and Collard. They reduce beetle damage.

- Spinach and Radishes. They are both able to repel leaf miners and radishes can grow safe and well when planted with spinach.

- Dwarf Zinnias and Cauliflower. Dwarf Zinnias are great because their nectar lures predatory insects like ladybugs; which are known to hunt down and eat common garden pests.

- Melons and Marigold. Marigold repels nematodes just as well as chemical treatments do.

- Love-in-a-mist and Strawberries. They are great for aesthetic purposes.

Chapter 5: Vegetables With Herbs

Many different vegetables grow well in gardens and having a vegetable garden can save you a lot of money on groceries. In terms of companion planting, certain herbs help to support the growth of vegetables by either improving soil quality or by attracting beneficial insects. In the chart below you will find several recommended planting combinations as well as information about specific benefits and any beneficial insects each combination attracts:

Plant Type	Recommended Companions	Benefits
Asparagus	Basil, tomatoes, parsley, dill, coriander, marigolds, aster flower	These plants all help to repel asparagus beetles. Basil helps to encourage ladybugs.
Beans	Cabbage, carrots, cauliflower, cucumber, celery, corn, marigolds, strawberries	Corn provides natural trellis and protection from the sun. Other vegetables help repel beetles.
Beets	Broccoli, sage, lettuce, onion	These plants help add minerals to the soil through the composting of leaves that contain magnesium.
Broccoli	Chamomile, celery, mint, rosemary, dill	Rosemary repels cabbage flies while dill attracts beneficial wasps to kill pests like the cabbageworm.

Cabbage	Beets, celery, bush beans, oregano, dill, onion, potatoes, mint, sage, chamomile, tomatoes	Aromatic plants/herbs help repel pests. Tomatoes help to deter diamondback moth larvae.
Carrots	Pole beans, bush beans, lettuce, onion, garlic, parsley, peas, radish, tomatoes, rosemary	Parsley, rosemary, and plants in the onion family repel carrot rust flies. Other plants attract predatory wasps and lacewings to control pests.
Cauliflower	Beans, celery, peas, oregano	Both peas and beans help to fix nitrogen in the soil.
Celery	Cauliflower, leeks, onion, cabbage, spinach, tomatoes	These plants help to improve soil quality and repel whiteflies.
Cucumber	Radishes, lettuce, spinach, garlic, chamomile, carrots, dill, beans, peas, sunflowers	Radishes help to repel cucumber beetles. Lettuce, spinach, and

		other greens repel whiteflies.
Eggplant	Potatoes, beans, spinach, peppers, marigolds	Beans help to repel Colorado potato beetles. Marigolds repel nematodes.
Leeks	Carrots, onions, strawberries, celery, celeriac	Celery prefers conditions similar to leeks and carrots repel leek moths.
Lettuce	Radishes, cucumber, strawberries, carrots, onions, broccoli, thyme, cilantro	These plants help to repel diamondback moth larvae.
Onion	Carrots, beets, dill, lettuce, strawberries, chamomile, marigolds, mint	These plants help to repel slugs, aphids, maggots, and beetles.
Peas	Garlic, turnips, cauliflower, mint	These plants help to repel Colorado potato beetles

Peppers	beans, okra, marjoram, tomatoes, sunflowers, onion, basil, clover	Ground-cover plants help increase humidity. Tomatoes can shelter fruit from sunlight.
Potatoes	Beans, marigolds, onion, peas, garlic, clover, thyme	These plants repel potato bugs and Mexican bean beetles.
Pumpkin	Jimson weed, catnip, oregano, tansy, radishes, buckwheat	These plants help repel squash bugs while radishes trap flea beetles.
Spinach	Peas, cauliflower, strawberries, beans, eggplant	Beans and peas provide shade for spinach. Radishes attract leaf miners away from spinach.
Tomatoes	Celery, spinach, asparagus, carrot, basil, parsley, garlic	Garlic protects against red spiders and basil can increase yield.
Zucchini	Flowering herbs	Flowering herbs attract bees to facilitate pollination.

Most herbs are very easy to grow, and they do well in all types of gardens, even container gardens. For herbs especially, container gardens are an excellent option because the herbs will continue to grow all year long if you simply move the container indoors when it starts to get cold. As is true for vegetables, there are certain planting combinations for herbs that are known to be beneficial. In the chart below you will find some recommended planting combinations as well as information about specific benefits and any beneficial insects each combination attracts:

Plant Type	Plant With	Benefits
Basil	Tomatoes, oregano, peppers, asparagus, grapes, petunias	When planted with tomatoes, basil is said to make the tomatoes taste better. These plants may help attract butterflies.
Catnip	Eggplant	Catnip helps to repel aphids, ants, and flea beetles.

Chamomile	Cucumber, onion, cabbage, most other herbs	Helps to increase essential oil production in other herbs.
Chives	Carrots, roses, grapes, tomatoes, carrots, broccoli, cabbage, mustard, apples	Chives repel carrot flies, cabbage worms, aphids, mites, and nematodes as well as apple scab.
Cilantro	Cabbage, lettuce, spinach, tomatoes, anise	Cilantro helps to repel aphids, whiteflies, dill potato beetles, and spider mites.
Dill	Broccoli, cabbage, corn, eggplant, fennel, lettuce, onions, cucumbers	Dill helps to attract honeybees and butterflies while repelling aphids, spider mites, squash bugs, and cabbage looper.
Fennel	Dill	Fennel helps to attract ladybugs and repels aphids.

Garlic	Beets, roses, tomatoes, cucumbers, lettuce, celery, cabbage, potatoes, peas	Helps to repel aphids, ants, cabbage looper, mites, maggots, slugs, diamondback moth larvae, etc. Planting with tarragon speeds growth for garlic.
Lavender	Lettuce, onion, chamomile, tomatoes, oregano, marjoram, sage, rosemary, basil, squash	Repels fleas and moths, may attract honey bees and butterflies.
Oregano	Tomatoes, peppers, grapes, pumpkin	Helps to repel aphids and can provide ground cover for pepper plants to increase humidity.
Parsley	Asparagus, tomatoes, corn	Attracts swallowtail butterflies and predatory wasps to protect tomatoes.

Peppermint	Cabbage, peas, tomatoes, garlic, onions, leeks, broccoli, cauliflower, Brussels sprouts	Helps to deter cabbage looper, aphids, cabbage root fly, ants, and onion fly.
Rosemary	Cabbage, beans, broccoli, cauliflower, carrots, thyme	Helps deter bean beetles and many other bean parasites.
Sage	Rosemary, cabbage, beans, carrots, tomatoes, marjoram, broccoli, cauliflower	Helps to attract honeybees and to repel cabbage flies, carrot flies, cabbage loopers, bean parasites.
Thyme	Cabbage, eggplant, cauliflower, broccoli, potatoes, strawberries, tomatoes, Brussels sprouts	Helps to deter cabbage worms, weevils, cabbage looper, whiteflies, and aphids.

Chapter 6: Insects In The Garden

There are millions of types of insects, but not all of them are pests determined to devour your crops. There are a lot of species that are referred to under the umbrella term of 'beneficial insects' which provide a natural form of pest control. For many gardeners, including myself, they are an essential part of organic and natural gardening.

Here are some of the most commonly found beneficial insects with information about what they eat and the environment they prefer.

Good Insects

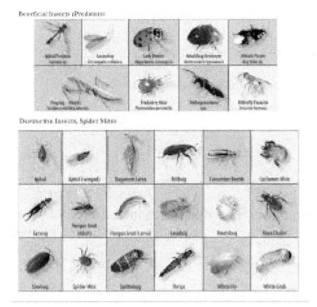

Ladybugs

These carnivorous insects feed on green and black aphids as well as red spider mites. Organic growers and gardeners love them, trying to attract these into their gardens. Every year ladybugs, or ladybirds as they are known in the UK, will lay hundreds of eggs. The larvae will eat thousands of aphids before maturing, hence the importance of providing a habitat for both this insect in both adult and larvae form. Typically, a ladybug will live for up to three years so long as it avoids being another predator's lunch!

Several plants attract ladybugs, including:

- Tansy

- Fennel
- Dill
- Cinquefoil
- Yarrow
- Alyssum
- Penstemon

Ladybugs feed on some common garden pests, including:

- Aphids
- Colorado potato beetles
- Fleas
- Mites
- Whitefly

Spiders

A surprising number of people don't like spiders, which is understandable as they aren't my favorite critter either. However, they are very useful in the garden as they eat a lot of different pests. Spiders will naturally find a home in your garden, but you can attract more to your vegetable plot.

Ground Beetles

These are your best friends as they are very voracious predators. These will eat almost anything, but are particularly fond of slugs and snails! Their eating habits will mean they won't get invited to the dinner table; they vomit on their prey, and the digestive enzymes start to dissolve their food.

Ground beetles are often killed by beer traps put down for slugs, as they walk along and fall in. Make sure there is a lip on your beer trap that will prevent these beneficial predators from drowning in the beer.

Most ground beetles are nocturnal and need somewhere shady to hide during the day. A pile of stones or logs or some leaf litter will give them a good place to hide out during the day.

Ground beetles are attracted to your garden by several plants, including:

- Clover
- Amaranthus
- Evening Primrose

The ground beetle will dine on many different pests, including:

- Slugs and snails
- Cutworms

- Colorado potato beetles
- Caterpillars

These are worth protecting and looking after in your garden because they will help to keep the pest levels down naturally.

Parasitic (Braconid) Wasps

These are very different from the wasps that bother a lot of gardeners. They tend to be smaller and will not sting you, unlike their bigger and more vicious cousins.

The lifecycle of these wasps is considered a little gruesome, but they benefit your garden in helping to control pest levels. This wasp will lay its egg in host insects. Once the egg has hatched, the larvae eat the host alive and then emerge as an adult. This family of wasps hunts many different pests including caterpillars, ants, aphids, and sawflies.

A wide variety of plants attracts parasitic wasps, including:

- Yarrow
- Dill
- Parsley
- Lemon Balm

- Lobelia
- Marigold
- Cosmos
- Alyssum
- Cinquefoil

They prey on a lot of different destructive insects, including:

- Aphids
- Caterpillars
- Tomato hornworm
- Tobacco hornworm

Damsel Bugs

Another great insect to attract into your garden, these are not fussy eaters and will prey on pretty much any insect that causes problems in your garden. In Europe, they live in orchards where they eat gypsy moths and red spider mites. This insect will overwinter in vegetation and appreciates somewhere to hide out between meals.

Damsel bugs are attracted to your garden by plants including:

- Alfalfa,

- Fennel
- Caraway
- Spearmint

They eat lots of common garden pests, including:

- Aphids
- Cabbage worms
- Caterpillars
- Corn earworms
- Leafhoppers
- Potato beetles
- Spider mites

By growing some ground cover and low-hanging plants, you can attract damsel bugs into your garden where they can help control pests.

Green Lacewings

These are particularly attractive insects that are common in British gardens. With their delicate, lacy wings you could be forgiven for thinking these innocent little creatures are of no use in your garden.

Don't be fooled by their good looks! These are voracious predators in both adult and larvae forms and will eat vast amounts of insect eggs and aphids. The larvae have large jaws which interlock to make pincers on which their prey is impaled. The larvae are very good at clearing your garden of soft-bodied pests.

Lacewings are attracted into your garden by several different plants, including:

- Angelica
- Coriander
- Cosmos
- Dandelion
- Dill
- Fennel
- Yarrow

Some of the insects eaten by lacewings include:

- Aphids
- Caterpillars
- Leafhoppers
- Mealybugs

- Whitefly

Soldier Beetles

Both adults and larvae are useful in pest control. The female lays her eggs in the soil where they overwinter, pupating in the spring. Therefore, you need to leave some areas of soil undisturbed to overwinter so these eggs can mature.

Soldier beetles also eat pollen, so pollen-bearing plants can help to attract them into your garden. Other plants that attract them include:

- Goldenrod
- Marigold
- Milkweed
- Wild lettuce
- Zinnia

These beneficial insects prey on many different insects, including:

- Aphids
- Caterpillars
- Corn rootworms
- Cucumber beetles

- Grasshopper eggs

These are interesting insects to look at and will help keep pests under control.

Tachinid Flies

Adult tachinid flies closely resemble the typical housefly and so are often mistaken for them. These are parasitic insects and lay their eggs in host insects. Depending on the species of fly, either eggs or live young are placed inside a host insect where they then eat their way out. Some species will even lay eggs on plants where host insects live which then hatch and eat them.

Tachinid flies can be bought, or you can attract them into your garden with a variety of plants including:

- Aster
- Buckwheat
- Carrots
- Cilantro (coriander)
- Chamomile
- Dill
- Fennel
- Feverfew

- Parsley
- Ox-eye and Shasta daisies

They prey on a lot of different pests, including:

- Caterpillars
- Colorado potato beetles
- Corn earworms
- Cutworms
- Earwigs
- Gypsy moths
- Japanese beetles
- Mexican bean beetles
- Sawfly beetles
- Squash bugs

Hoverflies

These are frequently confused with wasps as they share a black and yellow coloring, but they do not sting. They also hover (which wasps do not), do not have long antennae, and are typically smaller than stinging wasps. There are lots of different species of hoverflies, and they can fly as fast as 40km/h in short bursts.

Hoverflies will naturally find their way into your garden, but you can attract more of them with plants such as:

- Alyssum
- Cosmos
- Dill
- Lemon balm
- Mallow
- Marigold
- Yarrow

Hoverfly larvae prey on some garden pests including:

- Aphids
- Caterpillars
- Scale insects

Predatory Mites

Humid environments attract these mites such as polytunnels (hoop houses) and greenhouses, where they are most welcome as they prey on spider mites! Spider mites can be a serious problem in greenhouses and very hard to control.

Predatory mites can find their way into your greenhouse, but more often people will buy these beneficial insects and introduce them to the environment.

When there are no spider mites for them to feed on, they will feed on pollen from your plants, helping with pollination.

Solitary Bees

There are lots of species of solitary bee, which does not live in colonies, choosing to live by themselves instead. In Britain alone, there are over 200 different species of solitary bee, including the masonry bee, which is often mistaken for a hornet or wasp.

These bees can look like wasps or honeybees, but they are no threat whatsoever to you. The females dig nests, which are then stocked with food (nectar and pollen) and sealed. The young are left to fend for themselves. These bees will usually nest under the ground, often being found under sheds, in piles of logs, and so on. You can help encourage them to your garden by making an insect hotel.

These are vital pollinators and should be encouraged into your garden with flowering plants such as:

- Catnip
- Fuchsia
- Heather

- Lavender

- Marjoram

- Viburnum

You now know about some of the beneficial insects that you want to attract into your garden. Of course, there are many more insects, and some will depend on where in the world you live. In some areas praying mantis is a beneficial insect, but here in England, I won't ever see one in the wild.

Growing the right types of plants will help attract these insects into your garden and should be part of any gardener's plan. Chemicals should be avoided where possible because they indiscriminately kill both beneficial and harmful insects. With certain chemicals, the residue will persist for the rest of the growing season, which can prevent beneficial insects from returning.

Bad Insects

While the perfect garden would only attract beneficial insects that would prey on anything and everything that dared step foot into the garden, that's rarely the case. Most gardens contain a wide variety of insects, both good and bad.

Let's take a closer look at some of the more common pests found in gardens across the country. If you're lucky, you won't have to deal with more than one or two of these insects at once.

Aphids

Aphids, also known as plant lice, are tiny little insects that can quickly multiply into a huge problem that spans across the vast majority of a garden. A single aphid making its way into an unprotected garden can result in millions or even billions of aphids quickly populating every nook, cranny, and corner of your garden.

Aphids can have up to 12 live babies per day. Within the first week, one aphid can have 84 babies. Within a week those aphids are ready to start having babies of their own. The 84 babies will start adding 12 babies apiece per day, which is more than 1,000 aphids being added daily. Once they start having babies, the numbers jump even more dramatically. Within a month, millions of aphids will be infesting the garden. Of course, this simple scenario assumes no aphids die and that each of the aphids has exactly 12 babies per day, but you get the point.

Luckily, you have some options when it comes to controlling aphids. You can plant caraway, chamomile, dandelions, buckwheat, and tansy to attract insects that prey on them. Ladybugs, green lacewings, praying mantises and minute pirate bugs will all make a meal of aphids. Nasturtiums can be used as a trap crop for aphids.

Additionally, you can use the following plants to repel aphids

- Basil.
- Catnip.
- Chives.
- Clover.
- Coriander.
- Dill.
- Eucalyptus.

- Fennel.
- Garlic.
- Onions.
- Nettles.
- Peppermint.
- Radishes.

A combination of plants that attract insects that attack aphids and plants that aphids don't care for seems to be the best way to prevent aphids from making their way into the garden. If you catch an infestation while it's underway, use a strong spray of water to wash aphids away from your plants. Watch your plants closely after that and wash them down again if the aphids return.

Asparagus Beetles

Asparagus beetles are orange and white or blue-black beetles that prey on asparagus shoots. From larvae to mature adults, asparagus beetles will make a meal of both the leaves and the stems of the asparagus plant. Knock the larger beetles into a bucket of soap to get rid of them.

Ladybug larvae will eat both the eggs and the larvae of the asparagus beetle, so keep plants that attract ladybugs in your garden. Additionally, the following plants are known to deter asparagus beetles

- Basil.

- Coriander.

- Parsley.

- Petunias.

- Tomatoes.

Cabbage worms and Cabbage Loopers

Cabbage worms and cabbage loopers attack Brassica crops all across North America. They look like white or green caterpillars and will tunnel through the roots of cabbages.

Beneficial nematodes are the main predator needed in the garden to clear out cabbage worms. Nematodes will likely have to be purchased because they're difficult to attract. In addition to adding nematodes to the soil, the following plants can be grown to prevent cabbage worms from ever making their way into a garden:

- Borage.

- Celery.

- Dill.

- Radishes.

- Rosemary.

- Sage.

- Thyme.
- Tomatoes.

Another option is to plant a crop like mustard that attracts cabbage loopers and cabbage worms around the outside of your garden as a trap crop that can be sacrificed to protect more desirable crops.

Caterpillars

Caterpillars attack a wide range of plants, chewing on leaves, tunneling through fruit, and leaving droppings behind everywhere they go. While the butterflies some of them will eventually become may be beneficial to a garden, they're quite the pest while in the caterpillar stage. Of particular concern are cutworms and cabbage loopers, which have been known to quickly strip plants of their foliage.

To keep caterpillars at bay, add plants to your garden that draw in parasitic wasps, praying mantises, and green lacewings. Another option is to hang a bird feeder to call in birds that'll come for the bird food and supplement their meals with any caterpillars that cross their paths. When you see a caterpillar, handpick it and move it far from your garden.

The following plants can be planted in a garden to repel caterpillars:

- Lavender.
- Peppermint.
- Sage.

Colorado potato beetle

The Colorado potato beetle looks like a yellowish-orange ladybug with stripes instead of dots. While ladybugs are a preferred predator in the garden and will eat Colorado potato beetles, these pests will quickly defoliate peppers, potatoes, eggplant, and tomatoes. In addition to ladybugs, nematodes are beneficial to have around when potato beetles are present.

Some sources indicate the Colorado potato beetle doesn't like to walk over coarse mulch. Adding a layer of straw mulch around your plants may prevent the beetle from making it to your plants.

The following plants will repel Colorado potato beetles:

- Catnip.
- Chives.
- Coriander.
- Eucalyptus.
- Garlic.
- Green beans.

- Marigolds.
- Nasturtiums.
- Peas.

Flea Beetles

These tiny little pests are found across the entirety of North America. They chew small, round holes in the leaves of most vegetables and will jump around nervously when disturbed. Flea beetles prefer dry soil to lay their eggs in, so keep your soil damp to make your garden less attractive. Nematodes can be added to the soil to make short work of any larvae that do hatch.

The following plants will repel flea beetles:

- Catnip.
- Peppermint.
- Rue.
- Thyme.

Mealybugs

Mealybugs are tiny creatures that appear in clusters at the base of leaves. They'll attack a wide variety of fruit and vegetables, including citrus trees, grapes, and potatoes. They suck the sap out of plants and leave a honeydew residue behind that can quickly start to mold.

Lacewings and mealybug destroyers enjoy eating mealybugs, so do what it takes to attract them to your garden. Companion planting isn't an effective means of eliminating mealybugs.

Mexican bean beetle

The Mexican bean beetle is a connoisseur of many varieties of beans. It has a bottomless pit for a stomach and will continue chewing on the leaves of a plant until it starts to die. These beetles roam the Western half of the United States, looking for bean crops to devastate.

The following plants are known to repel Mexican bean beetles

- Garlic.
- Marigolds.
- Rosemary.

Japanese Beetles

Japanese beetles are commonly found in the Eastern half of the United States and are known to attack a variety of vegetables and flowers. They're a bluish-green color and feature rust-colored wing covers. They're pretty to look at, but the damage they can do to a crop is anything but pretty.

The following plants will deter Japanese beetles:

- Catnip.

- Chives.

- Chrysanthemums.

- Garlic.

- Marigolds.

- Onions.

- Rue.

Scales

Scales are aptly named because, at a glance, they look like small scales attached to a plant. They're destructive little creatures that will suck sap from plants during every stage of their life cycle. When you notice scales on your plants, prune them back to get rid of the affected areas or scrub them off the branches.

There are no plants that are known to deter scales, so you'll have to rely on predatory insects to get the job done. Ladybugs, praying mantises and green lacewings will all dine on scales, so plants that attract them may help.

Thrips

These tiny insects are so small you probably won't see them on your plants. What you will see are discolored areas that take on an almost silvery sheen as the thrips bite into the plants repeatedly and leave a large number of tiny little scars. Thrips aren't problematic unless the population gets out of control and begins to spread viruses. P

Tomato Fruitworms (Corn Earworms)

Tomato fruitworms, also known as corn earworms, cotton bollworms, and geranium budworms, are found in gardens throughout North America. These worms are known by several names, usually indicative of the type of plant they're attacking. They've been known to dine on cotton, beans, peas, peppers, tomatoes, corn, geraniums, potatoes, and squash.

The adults are small moths that lay eggs on the bottoms of leaves. The larvae feed on the leaves as they grow. If they're attacking a corn crop, they'll move into the husks as the corn matures and will eventually begin to feed on the silk and the corn kernels at the ends of the ears.

Geraniums and thyme are known to deter the tomato fruitworm.

Tomato Hornworm

This large caterpillar is found in gardens throughout the United States, usually munching on the leaves of eggplant, peppers, potatoes, and tomatoes. They develop into large moths that have a wingspan of up to 5".

The following plants will repel tomato hornworms:

- Borage.

- Dill.
- Thyme.

Chapter 7: How to Start Companion Planting

Once you know which plants you want to grow and what your primary goals for companion planting are, it's time to get your system into action.

Cost, Materials, Location, and Time

The cost of establishing a new garden can be quite variable, depending on some factors. First among them is whether you want to start your garden from seed or buy seedlings that are already somewhat established. Seeds are far less expensive than seedlings, but the advantage of the latter is that you can plant them right away in a prepared bed, instead of starting them indoors and transplanting them.

Assess your budget and how much time you want to commit to getting the garden started and base your decision on that. To maintain a companion garden, you don't need too many materials. A source of water is of course essential, whether it is a rain barrel, well pump, or spout. Beyond that, a sturdy spade, a garden rake or hoe, and a trowel are all you need to garden with.

These are the gardener's basic toolset, and with them, you can maintain any patch of the garden easily. While you can buy them new, if you are on a budget you can always look for them at garage sales or thrift shops. Make sure you are getting good quality, however – they will get a lot of use, and you don't want flimsy tools that will wear out easily. Locate your garden in an area that gets a lot of sun through the growing season. You can assess the sunlight simply by checking shadows throughout the day to see which areas get the lightest. Very simply, you do not want tall buildings or trees shading the area you will locate your garden in. Additionally, the garden should be in a well-drained area.

Do not locate your garden at the bottom of an elevated area that will flood it with rain runoff. And if you can locate it conveniently close to your house, it will make maintenance and harvest a much easier job. The amount of time you spend on your garden is also based on several factors, such as the size of the garden, how many different plants you are growing, and how eager you are to invest a lot of effort in maintaining it.

But the majority of your time will be spent on establishing the garden: one of the major benefits of companion planting is that it saves you a lot of time on a day-to-day basis. Since the plants are providing one another with nutrients, pest control, and weed control, you don't have to spend as much time performing these tasks yourself.

Be prepared to spend a few afternoons establishing your garden, and after you've done so, you won't have to spend more than an hour or two a week on watering, checking for pests and weeds, and monitoring the plants' growth and vitality.

Compost and Soil Maintenance

For starters, you will need to prepare productive, healthy soil. Whether you are adopting a new or unused piece of ground to a companion garden space, it can be tempting to try to finish the preparation phase as quickly as possible and get straight into production. But building soil with the right texture, with a good blend of different sized mineral particles and organic matter, will help ensure your plants have the best foundation to grow well.

Your companion garden will need rich, healthy soil to be fertile and productive. The amount of time you spend preparing the soil will pay off huge dividends in the long run, so it is certainly worth it. Your crops' vigor and overall health will be greatly affected by how effectively you prepare the soil. The most productive garden soil has 5-10% organic matter: this includes fallen bits of plant and animal detritus, decaying leaves, and humus.

While this amount does not seem particularly large, just a small amount of organic matter can go a long way to ensuring the soil is healthy. Decaying organic matter provides nutrients to the soil and improves its structure, creating a loose, crumbly loam that is easier for roots to move through. It helps small particles of clay bind together into larger pieces, which improves drainage, and it helps to hold water in the soil that would normally be dry, sandy, and infertile.

To build up the organic content of your garden bed, add about an inch of compost or well-finished livestock manure every year as an amendment to the soil. You can also add coarse mulch such as four inches of straw or dead leaves. If you have deep, raised beds, you will need to add more organic matter, and the same applies if you are working in a particularly hot climate, in areas that are heavily used, or if you have sandy or heavy soil.

It's also important to make sure the soil is properly aerated. This ensures that microscopic life can flourish, creating the right conditions for organic matter in the soil to be broken down into nutrients the plants can use. In a smaller garden, you can use a spade or spading fork to turn the soil. Loosen the top eight to twelve inches as much as you can, and work compost or manure into it as you do so. Use a hoe or a rake to break up clumps of soil and form a smooth, level surface.

If the soil in your garden is particularly heavy or rich with clay, you may want to consider renting a rotary tiller to break it up. These machines have churning tines that cut through dense soil. While they do not dig as deeply as you can with a spade, the depth they provide will usually be enough, particularly if you plan to establish raised beds. While renting a rotary tiller costs more than turning the soil by hand, you can usually finish the job more quickly with one. If your garden plot is particularly large, it can be well worth the investment.

Creating Gardens in Limited Spaces

In a companion garden, you can organize planting arrangements in many different ways, based on your goals and the amount of space you have. One of the major advantages of companion planting is that it allows you to get more out of smaller spaces because you can mix crops in ways that maximize the amount of space available.

Double Rows are a simple way to combine two types of crops. This is a great technique for growing bush beans or cucumbers alongside lettuce or other greens. This system allows you to grow a weed-suppressing canopy (or "natural mulch") that reduces the amount of work you have to do. Double rows are also a great way to plant climbing vegetables on either side of a trellis.

Wide Rows can be up to five feet across. This is just wide enough that you can reach the plants in the middle of the row from either side. This allows you to walk around the bed instead of on it, which will help prevent soil compaction. The broad growing area lets you plant several kinds of companion plants in a staggered formation or side by side across the row.

Wide rows are perfect for growing lots of small plants like leafy greens and root crops in a small area. You can interplant leaf lettuce, carrots, radishes, and onions in staggered rows in the spring. You can also grow larger plants in a wide row, with insect-repellent flowers around the outside.

Local Climate Conditions and What to Grow

Climate conditions can be astonishingly variable from one latitude to the next, and because of that, you must find out what hardiness zone you live in. Hardiness zones are geographically defined climate regions that have similar growing conditions throughout. They're generally arrayed along fairly well-defined latitudes but can be subject to the effects of geographical features such as mountains, large bodies of water, and local climate conditions.

All regions of the world have hardiness zone maps available that will tell you what is best to grow there as well as when local frost dates generally occur. Familiarize yourself with these frost dates as well as what plants are best suited to grow in your region's hardiness zone.

Different Methods

There are a few different companion planting methods that have been shown to work particularly well. You may have already heard of some of them. The three sisters' technique, square foot gardening, container gardening, and the seven-layer system known as the forest garden are some of the most popular.

The Three Sisters

This is a companion planting technique that was developed by Native Americans to enhance the growth conditions of some of their staple crops: corn, beans, and squash. This technique uses the companion methods of structural support and nutrient cycling. Three or four bean plants are planted around the base of each corn plant in rows, with squash planted between the rows. The beans fix nitrogen in the soil for the corn plants, which in turn provide structural support for the bean vines. The squash also benefits from the nutrient cycling of the beans, and its broad leaves provide natural mulch to shade out weed plants.

Square Foot Gardening

Square Foot Gardening is a companion technique designed to increase the amount of yield from a small garden space. In this method, long rows are abandoned in favor of a grid system. The grid is composed of 1' x 1' squares, and each square is dedicated to a different crop. This method allows the gardener to intercrop numerous cultivars in the same location more easily. This is useful because, with a square foot garden, you can incorporate companion plants, pest repelling flowers, attractive plants to lure pollinators and predatory insects, and cycle nutrients. This allows you to get the most effective companion planting system in the smallest space.

Container Gardening

This is a useful method for making the most of small spaces, as well as gardening when you only have a balcony, rooftop, or patio available to work with. You can apply any of the principles of companion planting to your container garden for pest control, nutrient cycling, and structural support just as you would if you were planting in the ground. An additional aspect of companion planting in containers is the fact that you have more spatial variability to work with. You can trail creeping vines from the edges of containers, especially if they are hanging baskets. And you can build successively taller layers in the container, working from the outside edge inwards.

Allelopathy: The Chemical Abilities Of Plants

Allelopathy refers to the chemical interaction between shrubs, trees, and their components with the ecosystem of your garden. This is a key determinant of the choice of crops that should be used especially trees in companion gardening. Picture this, one way your garden may be failing is when the trees near it are consuming some minerals in your garden thus making it poorer mineral-wise.

With this understanding, we will seek to get to the root of trees that must not feature in the farm due to Allelopathic reasons. The black walnut for instance is a menace in the gardens. It is a natural secretor of hydrojuglone. Hydrojuglone is not a toxic chemical until it is oxidized. When oxidized, it becomes juglone which is a toxic substance that kills off any plants in the vicinity. Note that the secretions can go for up to a five-meter radius circle and poison a huge part of your garden.

The leaves and the bark of the black walnut are also secretors of this substance. Similarly, dangerous trees include red oak, black cherry, cottonwood, wax myrtle, and sugar maple tree. The American sycamore tree is also an active releaser of the toxins. That said, it is, therefore, vital to keep your garden as far as possible from these trees to protect your crops from this poisoning.

If you have an existing garden with these toxins, there are steps that you may take to reduce the impact of these substances on your crops. The first thing here at play is to remove any leaves that fall from the said trees and keep the garden as clean as possible. As you locate your garden to the perfect spot, be sure to plant a buffer zone of neutral crops and trees in between the crops and the dangerous trees. One of the best buffer crops to plant here is the Kentucky bluegrass. Once planted, it will be an efficient absorber of these toxins and very few will make it to your garden.

The trees that may be planted in the buffer zone to help in reducing the effect of the poison are crabapple trees, pine, dogwood, buckeye. Birch, beech, and the white ash tree. Though frowned upon, there are many fruit plants such as apples, berries, and grapes that can thrive in the buffer zone.

Allelopathy is not always on the negative though. Luciana tree for instance has great additive features to the soils. This miracle tree increases the yield of corn and other related crops on the farm. It is one of the best alternative trees for companion gardening and it generally enriches the plants around it.

Allelopathy can refer to the positive or harmful effects that a particular plant can have on another, derived from the plant's (whether crop or weed species) release of natural biochemicals that are known as allelochemicals.

With that said, if you plan to create your garden following the companion gardening system, you have to be able to understand the relationship of different plants with one another. More importantly, you have to be able to deduce whether or not your plants are doing more harm than good to one another.

Unfortunately, there are no easy ways to determine or diagnose symptoms of allelopathy for your plants. But there are obvious ways to infer whether or not your plants suffer from allelopathy, such as when your plants tend to die despite ensuring ideal growing conditions. If this is the case, try replanting it immediately and observe closely if the fresh plant's health begins to decline still. If this is not the answer, observe surroundings to see if any plants could contain and release allelopathic toxins that are causing the problem.

If you do discover that you have warring plants, do not panic. You simply have to keep them apart so that they can peacefully coexist with one another. Soil quality could also be a factor. Heavier soil will usually hold the toxins longer and therefore give more opportunity for the toxin to reach your garden. Remedy this by making sure your soil is well aerated and that it is well-drained.

Chapter 8: Garden Techniques

You need to maintain your garden so that your plants are healthy and happy. When they are, they will reward you with a massive yield that will leave you harvesting a ton of delicious (and healthy) treats to add to your dinner table.

How to Fertilize Your Plants

Fertilizer is an important piece of making sure that your vegetables grow healthy and strong. However, many people seem to think that fertilizer is some kind of magic potion for plants. This results in two misinformed ideas. Some people think that fertilizer fixes all problems; instead of identifying issues such as overwatering or poor temperature, these gardeners increase the strength of their fertilizer and expect their plants to suddenly start looking healthy. The other issue is believing that more fertilizer is always a good thing. This is simply not true; in fact, it is the opposite that is true. Plants being overfed fertilizer may burn themselves by absorbing too many nutrients but more often too much fertilizer messes with the pH level of the soil and makes it so the plants can't absorb any nutrients. To avoid these problems, you should always stick to the directions printed on the labels of whatever fertilizer you are using and you should educate yourself on fertilizers in general.

There are two ways to apply fertilizer. Most indoor or raised bed gardeners use a liquid fertilizer. This is made by purchasing either a liquid mixture that is diluted with water or a mixture of raw materials which is then dissolved in water. This is sprayed or poured onto the soil around the plants. However, many outdoor gardeners prefer to go with a solid fertilizer that is mixed into the soil itself. One way of doing this is to mix fertilizer in with the soil as you are making rows but before anything has been planted. When done in this way, the fertilizer is mixed to be spread out throughout the soil but under the top few feet so that the plants' roots can find it as they grow. Another way is to pour a line of fertilizer along the side of the row.

The best way to determine how often and how much fertilizer to give your plants is to follow the instructions on the package. Many gardeners will start their plants off with a smaller dosage to see how they respond to it before mixing it stronger and stronger until it is at the level recommended on the package.

It should be noted that solid fertilizers don't need to be used every week. This is the scheduling for a liquid fertilizer, which I recommend for beginners because it is harder to make mistakes with it. You could overfeed your plants, but as long as you are following the instructions it is unlikely that you will. However, a solid fertilizer can prove harmful to your plants, as direct contact with the roots while they are still young could just straight out kill your plants. If you use a liquid fertilizer and you are careful to follow the instructions, this won't be a problem for you. You can always branch out and start experimenting with other kinds of fertilizers after you get a feeling for how fertilizer changes the pH level of the soil and affects your vegetables. Just remember not to apply fertilizer directly to the plants but rather to the soil around them.

Watering Your Vegetable Garden

Watering the plants is another image that pops into people's minds when they think about gardening. Everyone knows that plants need water, though it seems that not everybody realizes just how much. Hydrogen is one of the macronutrients that plants need to live but too much hydrogen causes root rot and leaves your plants sick.

Too little water also leaves them sick, though it is typically better to err on the side of too little than too much. Your plants use visual signs to communicate their needs to you. One of the clear ways that plants tell us they need water is to start wilting. However, before you go watering them, you need to make sure that the reason they are wilting is the lack of water. If you notice your plants are wilting around noon, avoid watering them right away. This is the time of day when the sun is at its hottest and it may be the heat that is causing the wilt. Wait a couple of hours and see if your plants bounce back as the temperature cools off. If they don't, then they probably do need watering. If they do bounce back, wilting was a part of the way that the plants withstand their environment. Midday wilting is the plant equivalent to people sweating a lot in the heat.

Of course, underwatering your plant can also easily kill it but most gardeners don't have a problem with underwatering. It is overwatering that does the most harm, especially to beginners who haven't done their research. If you want to be a gardening pro, then you need to get used to doing research. It takes next to no time and it can stop you from making deadly choices.

How often you should be watering your vegetables is going to be determined by four factors: the soil you are using, the temperature of your local climate, whether your plants are getting full sun or shade, and the species of plants you are growing. Oftentimes you can collapse those last two factors together because a vegetable needs a specific amount of sun or shade but there is enough variation there to make it worth the extra note. We'll discuss how these factors interact before moving on to how to tell it is time to water and how to properly water your plants when they are ready.

There is a true method that gardeners have been using for centuries to solve this exact problem. All you need to do to tell if it is time to water your vegetables is stick a finger in the soil.

This is called the finger test. Stick a finger an inch into the soil and see if you feel any moisture. You might not but this doesn't mean there isn't any. Pull your finger out and give it a look. If it is clean then the plants are dry enough to be watered. If the soil is sticking to your finger then this means that it is still moist and you should wait another day or two before watering. As simple as that is, it is the best and most accurate way to tell if it is time yet or not.

If it is time, you are best off watering your plants earlier in the day than later. This will give more time for the water to drain through the soil or evaporate back into the atmosphere. While not all of the water is going to leave this quickly, it beats watering in the late afternoon or at night when the colder temperatures are more likely to keep moisture trapped in the soil threatening the health of your plants.

Weeding Your Garden

When it comes to maintenance, you've probably noticed that fertilizing and watering your garden isn't a lot of work. You only fertilize once a week and you only water about twice a week. It would be great if growing your delicious vegetables was this easy but the real hardship comes in weeding your garden.

Weeds are simply plants that spread naturally and don't belong in your garden. Weeds are notoriously fast-growing plants and can very quickly take over a garden bed if left unchecked. They then steal energy from your plants by using the nutrients and water that would normally be used by your veggies. Large weeds or a mass of them are also able to block rays of light from breaking through to your plants. All and all, they want to leave your plants dead and take over the garden to call their own. If you are to have any chance of stopping them before they do this, you need to learn to identify them when they first arrive.

Set Up Shade

Although you may be growing plants that love direct sunlight, there may be moments when the heat is too much for them. When faced with a heatwave, these plants may get burned or damaged. You should be checking the weather not only every day but also the extended forecast. If there are spikes in the temperature, you may need to set up shade for your plants. This isn't done to reduce the amount of sun the plants are getting.

Add Mulch to Your Garden

Mulching your garden means adding a layer of material to the top of your garden. Popular materials for mulch are grass clippings, straws, shredded bark, sawdust, woodchips, shredded newspaper, cardboard and so much more. When it comes to gardening, the best mulch you can use is straw. This layer helps slow the drainage of the top part of the garden bed and makes it harder for weeds to take hold as seeds are much more likely to get trapped in the mulch layer rather than get into the soil properly. This also helps keep your plant's roots cooler, which can help during heat waves. Mulching can be done for aesthetic reasons too, as a colored mulch can make your landscaping pop. Add mulch to your garden after your seedlings have grown at least two sets of leaves. Keep an eye on your mulch and replace it as it begins to decompose.

Chapter 9: The Key to Switching to Companion Planting

In the most basic sense, companion planting is the technique of combining two or more plants for a particular purpose. The most common reason is for pest control, although there are other very useful benefits to companion planting as well. While some methods of companion planting can benefit your garden in several different ways, and depending on what you want to grow, you can choose to concentrate on one or all these areas:

Insects

Companion planting helps keep your plants free of harmful insects in three ways. First, insects are often attracted to their preferred crops by their sense of smell. For example, cabbage worms are attracted to their favored host plants by the mustard oils in them. And onion maggots find onions by following the sulfur compounds released by the plant.

One way you can use companion planting to protect your plants is to mask their odors with other fragrant smells. Plants like garlic, for example, release aromas into the air that can deter bean beetles and potato bugs. Onions can keep pests from attacking strawberries or tomatoes. Mint can "hide" cabbage from cabbage loppers, while basil can do the same thing to keep hornworms away from your tomatoes.

By edging your garden with pungent plants, as well as mixing them into your garden, you can have a natural insect repellent growing among your vegetables. Some plants are almost irresistible to certain pests, and you can use these to lure them away from your crops. Nasturtiums, for example, are a wonderful attractant because aphids simply love them.

Color potato beetles will prefer black nightshade to even your potato plants. Attractant plants can help to keep your crops free of pests in two ways, not only do they lure pests away from your desirable crops, but they also help to concentrate them in a location that will help make it easier to control them. Once these pests have been trapped on your decoy attractants, you can remove these plants and destroy them along with the pests.

The third way companion plants can help keep your garden free of pests is by making your garden attractive to beneficial insects. Growing dill, for example, will attract pest-eating insects such as lacewings and parasitic wasps, all of which will help control aphids, beetles, and caterpillars.

Nutrients

The soil in your garden is the source of all the nutrients your plants need to grow, and you must make sure it is healthy and rich to ensure a good harvest. There are various ways you can build good soil.

And while you can establish healthy soil by adding organic materials to it, building compost, and laying down mulch, you can also actively use companion planting to help maintain your soil's nutrient content through the growing season and from one year to the next. One of the most important nutrients plants need to grow well is nitrogen.

Many plants require more nitrogen while they are growing than any other nutrient. Nitrogen is vital to the production of chlorophyll and the process of photosynthesis. Because of this, you will find that most fertilizers contain a large amount of nitrogen. Certain plants – in particular, legumes – are nitrogen fixers. This means that they contain bacteria in their roots that help to convert unusable forms of nitrogen to forms plants can uptake and use.

By growing these plants among those that use a lot of nitrogen, you can help keep nitrogen levels in your garden more stable. Most plants that are nitrogen fixers are in the legume family, such as soybeans, alfalfa, peanuts, and clover.

Structural Support

There are several types of plants that need structural support to grow, and while many gardeners erect trellises or frames for them to grow on, you can also grow structural supports for these plants. Beans and other plants that grow on vines can be grown with sunflowers or corn as companions. By planting a few beans around the base of each corn or sunflower plant, you can grow a natural trellis that the bean plants can climb.

This has the additional benefit that beans, being nitrogen fixers, will help benefit the corn and sunflower plants as they grow. Structural support is not limited to climbers, however. It extends below the ground and can be considered in terms of shade and shelter as well. You can intercrop or plant your garden in a way that maximizes the efficiency of the garden space by increasing the yield in a smaller amount of space and making the most of water.

You can do this by mixing many different types of vegetables, but the goals should be to grow crops that will not be in direct competition with one another, especially if you are growing them in a smaller space. One way you can do this is by growing taller vegetables alongside shorter, shade-tolerant ones. Or, vegetables that have deep roots can be planted along with those with shallow roots. This minimizes competition for water and nutrients and has the added benefit of keeping the soil aerated at all levels.

Extended Harvest

This is one of the more difficult benefits to realize in terms of companion planting because it requires a bit more planning and forethought than some of the others. By planning out your garden with an eye to the life cycles and growth periods of the plants in it, you can dramatically extend its life from the early spring to the late fall and even into the winter. This is a sort of temporal (or time-centered) companion planting, in which new plants are cycling into the garden as others are dying or being harvested.

Everyone is familiar with the fact that tulips, daffodils, and other spring perennials are some of the first flowers you see after the snow melts. But they appear only briefly and are soon replaced by annuals and other plants that grow from seed through the late spring and summer. Because of this, many gardeners will plant bulbs in the same part of their garden that they intend to later fill with annual flowers like marigolds and black-eyed Susans. The same concept can be applied to your vegetable garden, as well.

You can plant cold-season vegetables such as cabbage and beets early in the spring (particularly if you grow them under a cold frame) before you have even started your warm-season vegetables indoors. Then, as the soil warms, you can plant a different set of crops where you are harvesting your cold season crops.

As fall approaches, you can replant another crop of cold-season vegetables in the same spot. In doing this, you extend the harvest of your vegetable garden considerably and allow it to produce a much greater yield than it would if you were only planting a single kind of vegetable for a short period of growing time.

You can concentrate more on one of these areas than the others if It is your first-time trying companion planting, or you can try to balance your garden to incorporate all of them. Once you have more experience with companion planting, you will be able to plan a garden that seamlessly balances insect control, nutrient cycling, structural support, and extended harvests, giving you better yields with less work.

Transitioning to a Companion Garden

Adding Companion Plants to an Existing Garden

If you have already got a well-established garden and you do not want to mess with it too much, you can still benefit from companion planting practices. You can begin the transition towards a companion-planted garden by adding a few beneficial species to your existing garden.

Rather than changing your garden plan in one fell swoop, you can start by working with what you already have. Perennials such as asparagus can benefit from the addition of some companion vegetables and herbs. You can plant flowers and herbs around the borders and between the rows of your garden. Maybe as a first project, you can dismantle your onion patch and plant onions amongst your other vegetables. Every year you will get a little more comfortable with companion planting, and you will become an expert on what works best in your garden.

It also helps to think outside the box or the garden plot. You may not think of your raspberry bushes or your crab-apple tree, much less your flower beds, as part of your vegetable garden. But these areas also benefit from companion planting.

- Alliums: This is the family that includes onions, garlic, and chives. Plant these throughout your garden rather than keeping them all together. They will deter a wide variety of insect pests while at the same time attracting beneficial insects. Just keep them away from beans, peas, and sage. Chives produce attractive (and edible) flowers and can be used in flower gardens too. They are often used to protect roses from black spots, but the chives must be established for a few years before you will get results.
- Aromatic Herbs: Basil, oregano, mint, dill, rosemary, and sage will keep a variety of flying insects at bay, so you can

plant them throughout and around your garden. Mint can take over very quickly, so It is best to keep it in a container. Dill should be kept away from carrots.

- Marigolds: Plant some of these throughout your garden. You can even scatter the seeds to the wind in early spring and let them pop up where they will. French marigolds produce a natural pesticide in their roots that can keep soil pests such as nematodes at bay. The scent of the marigold plant also deters flying insect pests.
- Nasturtiums: These can repel squash bugs, and act as a trap crop for aphids. You can plant them amongst your squash, or adjacent to the crops that you are trying to protect from aphids. Nasturtiums are beautiful to look at and are also edible. The peppery leaves and bright flowers add flavor and color to salads.
- Radishes: These have a couple of advantages. You can interplant them in your garden because they mature while many of your other plants are still growing. They also act as a trap crop for a variety of insect pests. Little-known fact: radish seed pods are delicious raw or cooked if you pick them green!
- Zinnias: Plant some of these colorful annuals around the edges of your garden or between the rows to attract beneficial insects to your garden. Pollinators such as wasps,

hoverflies, and a wide variety of butterflies are attracted to zinnias.

More Tips for Transitioning to Companion Planting

If you have raspberries, try planting turnips and garlic near them. Garlic deters fungus and Japanese beetles, while turnips will repel Harlequin beetles.

If you have asparagus, you know how long it took you to establish it. It is not going anywhere, but you can plant some tomatoes, parsley, and basil around it. Just keep the onions, garlic, and potatoes further away.

Do you have an apple or other fruit trees? Instead of leaving the ground underneath them bare, you can plant herbs such as chives or bee balm. Chives can have the same protecting effect on apples as they do on roses. Bee balm is great for attracting pollinators and other beneficial insects. You can plant flowers such as Echinacea and lupins under fruit trees as well. Echinacea helps make deep soil nutrients more available to the trees, and lupins are nitrogen fixers that also attract butterflies.

Start adding vegetables to your flower beds. Flowering herbs such as chives and oregano are an obvious place to start, but even peppers, eggplants, and cherry tomatoes can look attractive in a flower bed. If your flower garden incorporates a fence, use it as a trellis for scarlet runner beans. These edible beans have also long been used as decorative plants because of their brilliant red flowers.

Chapter 10: Mistakes to Avoid

Starting Too Big

One of the most common mistakes that you should never attempt to do is to start big with companion gardening. Even if you have a big lawn or backyard intended for this purpose, you should always try a smaller plot first.

Consider your first plot as an experimental plot. When you have a smaller plot, you can manage it well and also observe if the plants that you have paired work. After all, since you intend to produce crops for personal use, then it could be best to have plots that you can readily manage rather than have several plots that you can't carefully attend to. It's a bad picture if you have plants dying in front of you.

Not Preparing Your Soil

No matter how good the pair of plants that you intend to put into your garden, your labor will never bear much fruit if you have poor soil. Soil is the key to growing good produce, as plants typically are dependent on it for most of the nutrients necessary for plant growth, development, and propagation. Before starting your companion garden, you should prepare the soil.

First, the removal of weeds, rocks, and other unwanted debris is important as it may interfere with the optimal growth of your plants. Weeds may compete, not only for space but also for available minerals in the soil that may hinder or retard your crop's growth. It is also helpful if you study the profile of the soil in your garden so you can estimate also how much water will be necessary.

Clayish soils are gummy-like in appearance and when you hold them, the lumps are very visible. Such soil does not promote good air and water circulation and is not healthy for companion gardening.

Sandy soils, characterized by too many grains and breaking easily, also are not advisable for companion gardening as it allows water to drain easily. This may leave your plants wilting as water provided to them may not be absorbed readily by the roots as the grains of the sand are too fine to hold water molecules in place. Apart from draining water easily, sandy soils often have low nutrient concentration and are also unlikely to promote healthy crops.

Regardless of whether the soil in your garden is clayish or sandy, you can improve it by mixing compost into it. Decayed organic matter typically makes up the compost added to soils. It is a good source of nutrients for plants and at the same time improves the quality and texture of the soil. You can readily produce your compost by allowing leaves, peels, and other biodegradable items to degrade.

Composting is done simply by creating a layer of biodegradable items then covering it with soil. This is performed alternatively, then the compost pit is watered regularly to hasten degradation. Compost may also alter the pH of the soil and so it is important that you also measure this factor. Most plants grow optimally in neutral soil (pH 7) and others like camellias and rhododendrons prefer a soil of acidic pH. Lilacs and clematis also favor a more basic soil. Keeping this in mind helps to augment your success in companion gardening.

Establishing Plots in Shady Areas

Another thing to avoid in companion gardening is to position your garden in the shady sector of the lawn or the backyard. Though other gardeners think of their convenience first when establishing their home plots, this is very beneficial in terms of achieving your goal of producing good quality crops or flowers. This is because sunlight is an important ingredient in a plant's physiological functions. The food-producing mechanism of plants can only be possible when sunlight is present. Though the requirements of plants for sunlight appear to vary, over-shading has never been known to help in crop production. Choose a site that is relatively exposed to the sun at the peak of the day.

Excessive Watering

It's good to water your plants once established in the plots, but it is never fruitful to have garden plants watered excessively. Too much water may soak the roots and endanger them (as it may promote root rot) or it may destroy sensitive parts like buds and new leaves promoting early abscission. Fungal diseases like lights and powdery mildew are also associated with overwatering.

It is best to study the water requirements of the plants that you plant in your companion garden. For reference as to whether there's a need to water your garden or not, you can stick your finger on the soil (up to the second knuckle) and if the soil is dry, you may water the plants. However, if it is still wet, there is no need to add water to the soil. You should also avoid watering the plants from above

If possible, water it below the stem so that it ensures faster root absorption of available water and prevents wastage. Control the pressure when you water your garden. Too much pressure may not only break off some parts of the plants but will also promote soil erosion and root exposure.

Conclusion

Thank you for making it to the end. With this book as a guide, you can enjoy the benefits of companion planting to make your garden healthier and more productive, and without having to work as hard to repel pests or keep your crops robust. Starting with a solid foundation of healthy soil that is rich in organic matter, carefully plan out how to arrange your companion garden to get the most out of your space.

Companion planting is receiving a lot of attention from the scientific community because it can help reduce the need for harmful chemicals in farming. Home gardeners are re-discovering this information and using it to their benefit.

Remember that increasing yield is not just about spatial efficiency, but also about extending the growing season to be as long as possible. By applying the principles of companion planting, you can have a beautiful, productive garden that takes care of itself. Companion planting is an important way to shift to using more sustainable, organic methods of keeping your garden healthy.

The key to successful companion planting is properly planning where the plants in your garden are going to go. You've got to carefully consider how each of the plants in your garden is going to interact with one another and then place them in the best possible locations to take advantage of those interactions. The biggest limitation regarding companion planting is the knowledge of the gardener. Arm yourself with as much knowledge as possible before you ever put on your gardening gloves.

Keep in mind that one of the most common mistakes that you should never attempt to do is to start big with companion gardening. Even if you have a big lawn or backyard intended for this purpose, you should always try a smaller plot first.

Assess your budget and how much time you want to commit to getting the garden started, and base your decision on that. To maintain a companion garden, you don't need too many materials.

A source of water is of course essential, whether it is a rain barrel, well pump, or spout. Beyond that, a sturdy spade, a garden rake or hoe, and a trowel are all you need to garden with.

Remember that in Companion planting, there are millions of types of insect, but not all of them are pests determined to devour your crops. There are a lot of species that are referred to under the umbrella term of 'beneficial insects' which provide a natural form of pest control. For many gardeners, including myself, they are an essential part of organic and natural gardening.

Once you know which plants you want to grow and what your primary goals for companion planting are, it's time to get your system into action. This book will explain how to get started with companion planting in the real world – taking your plans and making them a reality in your garden.

By weaning your garden off of chemical fertilizers and insecticides, and using natural methods to keep your plants healthy and free of pests, you will be improving not only your plants' health but your own as well. You'll also be improving the environmental and carbon footprints. And your garden will be more robust as a result and better equipped to handle various weather conditions, droughts, and disease. Good luck!

CPSIA information can be obtained
at www.ICGtesting.com
Printed in the USA
LVHW051159100621
689885LV00002B/169